920 4151

THREE BODLEY HEAD MONOGRAPHS

GENERAL EDITOR: KATHLEEN LINES

THREE BODLEY HEAD MONOGRAPHS

Henry Treece
MARGERY FISHER

C. S. Lewis
ROGER LANCELYN GREEN

Beatrix Potter
MARCUS CROUCH

THE BODLEY HEAD
LONDON SYDNEY
TORONTO

808
.06
HEN

SBN 370 00798 0

Henry Treece © Margery Fisher 1969
Henry Treece's 'Notes on Perception and Vision'
© Mary Treece 1969
C. S. Lewis © Roger Lancelyn Green 1963
Beatrix Potter © Marcus Crouch 1960
Printed and bound in Great Britain for
The Bodley Head Ltd
9 Bow Street, London WC2
by C. Tinling & Co. Ltd, Prescot
Set in Monotype Ehrhardt
'Henry Treece' first published 1969
'C. S. Lewis' and 'Beatrix Potter' first
published, in two individual volumes, 1963
and 1960 respectively
This edition, revised and re-set, 1969

Henry Treece

MARGERY FISHER

ACKNOWLEDGMENTS

This monograph could not have been written without the help and approval of Mrs Henry Treece, who gave me access to her late husband's papers and generously put much time at my disposal to answer questions about him.

My thanks are due also to Mrs Jill Black of the Bodley Head and Miss Phyllis Hunt of Faber and Faber for allowing me to read and make use of the letters they exchanged with Henry Treece; to John Johnson, for many years Treece's literary agent, for permission to use his files and for bibliographical information; to Miss Esmé Green, Librarian to the Child and Youth Department of the Nottinghamshire County Library, Miss Janet Hill, Borough Children's Librarian of Lambeth, and F. T. Baker, Director of Lincoln City Library, for describing to me occasions on which Henry Treece gave talks to children; to Leonard Clark, for information about Treece's attitude to poetry and to teaching; to G. S. Fraser, for his views on and recollections of the Apocalyptic movement and Treece's contribution as a poet and anthologist; to Miss Enid Brooke, who made available to me her paper on Henry Treece and a check list of his works, prepared for the Department of Librarianship, Manchester College of Commerce, which provided a number of starting points; and to Miss Sally Morse, whose typing of the bibliography and of the notes on Perception and Vision from Treece's own MS enabled a deadline to be met.

My debt to Antony Kamm is great, for his advice, encouragement and active help, and for the direct contribution he had made in compiling the bibliography and in editing and arranging the notes and drafts of Henry Treece's last lecture, which are published here. Antony Kamm was a personal friend of Henry Treece, and as editor worked closely with him on many of his children's books, including all those published by the Brockhampton Press. They corresponded regularly for the last eight years of Treece's life, and I have been able to use freely the letters that passed between them.

I

Every man stands tall on the child he once was. The clamour
of Saturday night markets and the gloom of ruined castles
helped to make the pattern of Henry Treece's Black Country
boyhood. He was born at Wednesbury in Staffordshire in
1911. His father's family had lived in the same area of
Nottinghamshire at least from the late sixteenth century.
His mother's people migrated from Wales to the Midlands,
where his great-grandfather William Mason was connected
with an early Quaker iron-foundry. That ideal companion
for a boy, a reminiscent grandfather, had a store of tales of
local worthies, among them the pugilist known as the Tipton
Slasher. This same grandfather kept a sword hidden in the
ivy at the side of the house; Henry Treece remembered in
later years that it had great meaning for him although he
knew even then that it was eaten with rust and would fall
to pieces if he tried to use it.

There was another sword at Manchester, the town which
became the second focal point of his childhood—a sword
priced £5 and totally desirable to the child who pressed his
nose to the shop-window to gaze at it. Memories of Manchester and visits to relations were gathered in a broadcast
Treece gave in 1950; among tramcars, shops and cobbles
there was one figure he never forgot:

'Walter was a drayman who had stables somewhere near
Back Kay Street; not very far from a public-house and a
bank and a big shop which always had one of those rubber
tyre-men in the window. Walter was a big man, with a
proper walrus moustache that hung down splendidly, and
a body shaped like a pear, the heavy end downwards. He

7

had a triangular piece of cloth let into the top of his trousers, at the back, and a mare named Nelly, a great silly love of a thing with a rump like tawny plush. And he used to take sacks and sacks of flour out on his lorry, all over Manchester and as far out as Cheshire.'*

Sometimes casually, sometimes with mock reluctance, Walter would swing the boy into the driving seat and away they would go on journeys always fascinating, rain or shine, though the sheltering flour-bags left 'a mass of wet paste' on the shoulders by the end of the journey.

It was in Manchester, too, that the boy poked about a bookseller's shelves on a misty November afternoon and:

'. . . out of the dun-coloured book with the brown pages leapt up the words:
"Was this the face that launched a thousand ships
  And burnt the topless towers of Ilium. . ."
I shut the book, suddenly dazed and bewildered, and groped in my pockets for its price. I paid my ninepence and went out again into the Oxford Road. But now the mist had gone, and the cold was as a sweet Spring breeze; and I walked like a young Paris among the lights and ladies of the citadel.'†

The books Henry Treece was given as a child were mainly historical 'with lots of colourful pictures'; among them a melodramatic tale of Dick Turpin, a super-romantic King Arthur and a 'Technicolor Epic' of the Middle Ages by Queen Marie of Roumania.

In spite of Treece's early interest in history, his special subject at Wednesbury High School for Boys was literature; he spent much time also in the Art Room and all through his life enjoyed drawing and sketching. He won a scholarship

* No. 4 in 'Portraits of Cities : Manchester', broadcast Sunday, March 19, 1950.
† Ibid.

to Birmingham University, where he read English, History
and Spanish, graduating in 1933. At Birmingham he contributed verse to the university magazine and acted in dramatic
society productions, as well as captaining the University
boxing team. Training and practice in literature were coloured always by history. During his long career as a teacher
the plays were usually historical and he would always
emphasise this aspect of Shakespeare.

Treece's work seemed at first to lie mainly in the scholas-
tic world. His first post, in 1934, was in Leicestershire
Home Office school for delinquents at Shustoke. He moved
from here after a short time to The College, Cleobury
Mortimer, where he stayed for a year, until the school
closed. Here he met Mary Woodman, who was teaching
Geography at the school; they were to marry in 1939.
During this period Treece was writing a great deal of poetry
and after his next move, to Tynemouth School for Boys,
his poems began to find their way into the little magazines.
In September 1938 he moved from Tynemouth to the
Grammar School at Barton-on-Humber. This Lincolnshire
town was to be his home for the rest of his life, with one
break; his children were born in the country—David (who
died in infancy) in 1945, Jenny in 1947 and Richard in 1949.

Treece's teaching career was interrupted by the war. He
joined the Volunteer Reserve of the Royal Air Force as an
acting Pilot Officer and attained the rank of Flight-Lieuten-
ant. His eyesight was not of a standard to qualify him to fly.
He took a course as a navigator but served mainly as Intelligence Officer to 5 Group. After the war he returned
to the school at Barton-on-Humber as Senior English
Master. He held this last teaching post until his second
attack of coronary thrombosis in December, 1959, when he
was advised by his doctor that he should not go on trying to

combine two full-time careers. He made the difficult choice and retired from teaching to give himself entirely to writing.

In the years at Tynemouth immediately before the war poetry had come to dominate his writing life. He had met men directly concerned with the new verse of the time. Michael Roberts, Dylan Thomas, Herbert Read and others contributed to the enthusiasm which lay behind Treece's initiation with J. F. Hendry, of a literary movement, the New Apocalypse. One aspect of this movement must have been associated with the work of Dylan Thomas, for his approach to imagery was congenial to Treece. The two of them became friends through correspondence about their work and Treece's *Dylan Thomas; dog among the fairies*, published in 1949, was the first book to be written about this poet.

The New Apocalypse was consciously a militant movement, not only because most of its members at the start were in the Forces but, far more, because it represented a deliberate reaction against the political manifestos of the 1930s, the proletarian elements in the work of Auden, Spender and Day Lewis; equally, it was a movement away from surrealism and towards a direct relation to the actual world. At least one of the Apocalyptic poets, J. F. Hendry, believed the group should be partly political, standing for 'the restoration of order to myth, a pattern of myth, individual and social, which in art should correspond to planned socialism.'* But Treece's many definitions of the aims of the group, particularly in the collections entitled *Transformation*, suggest that he at least was making a straightforward attempt to expand man's horizons; perhaps most of all he and his friends were reacting against the oppression of the full personality by totalitarian ideologies and the repeated shocks and deprivations of war. A statement in

* *The White Horseman* (Routledge, 1941) p. 176.

How I see Apocalypse (1946), shows how broad and general Treece's view of the movement was:

'Apocalyptic writing, then, is the art form of the man who can recognise, without fear, the variety and multiplicity of life; of the man who acknowledges his dreams and his laughter, and the tiny and almost unmentionable things of life, as being real and desirable for sanity's sake. And the Apocalyptic attitude will teach Poetry to be broad, deep, limitless, like true life. It will teach men to live more, and exist less; it will be militant against all narrow, shallow, half-thoughts and back-door sniggerings. Such poetry will burn with a great fire, intensely, and out of that fire will spring a remoulded life, strong, happy, prophetic, scorched free of dross and cruelty.'*

During the war Treece helped to edit several anthologies, among them *The White Horseman* and *The Crown and the Sickle* (1944), which set out to show by example the Apocalyptic aims. In fact the New Apocalypse seems to have been a loose association of young poets, most of them living in the provinces and needing the stimulus of like-minded writers. Looking back on those years, G. S. Fraser says, 'The Association begun by Hendry and Treece enabled us to reach across space, and to correspond with other poets of whose existence we had not known.'† Undoubtedly the anthologies provided a platform and an audience for poets who might not otherwise have been able to surmount the difficulties of those years.

During the war years the movement lost its coherence. Treece's poetry was now being published by Faber's through his friend T. S. Eliot. He edited an anthology of Air Force poetry with John Pudney and made a more deeply personal working alliance with Stefan Schimanski,

* *How I see Apocalypse* (Lindsay Drummond, 1946) p. 80.
† In an interview with Antony Kamm, 1969.

whom he met early in the war. The anthologies they compiled together included the *Transformation* volumes of prose and verse in which writers like Herbert Read and Stephen Spender developed stimulating literary theories.

The Apocalyptic vision had not waned, although the time for defining it had passed. Treece's conception of man is consistent all through his work. On June 1, 1966 he attended a Symposium at the School of Fine Art at Hull's Regional College of Art and Crafts and addressed students on 'Perception and Vision.' His talk, the last he was to give, seems to light up the purpose and the achievement of his life and to demonstrate once and for all the balance in him of poet and novelist.*

In an introduction to *The White Horseman* G. S. Fraser, stressing the differences between the poets represented in that anthology, had described Treece's poems as 'a rich, elaborate world, in which you can lose yourself.'† He pointed out the Spenserian element in them—the fairy-tale atmosphere, the ornamental, almost allegorical writing. Indirectly he was stressing their preoccupation with the past. Treece's poetry, he wrote, '. . . is like a child's conception of time, all the past a sort of "once upon a time" world, where the heroes of different stories might meet and talk to each other.'

Treece has been variously defined as a poet who took to prose or a prose writer who began by writing poetry. It seems idle to separate the two aspects of his art, however sharply divided they might be technically. When he stopped writing poetry in the early 1950s he said more than once that the stream had dried up. It would seem, rather, to have been diverted. In his poetry two components of his novels —story and image—are pre-eminent. In 1946 he wrote:

* Extracts from his own notes for this lecture are printed on pp. 85-97 of this monograph.
† *The White Horseman*, p. 20.

'The most primitive use of the word is as an image, a word which, with or without the help of an epithet, conveys a mental picture of the object mentioned.'*

and later, suggesting the possible course of post-war poetry:

'. . . there are those who believe that narrative poetry will return in full force . . . If this were so, it would follow that the images employed would be those best suited to the flow of a story, which would not impede, or even, of themselves, heighten the effects of a tale whose principal interest would lie in its *action*.'†

The forecast of a return to narrative poetry was not in fact fulfilled; poets turned to shorter, more enigmatic forms. Fashion did not turn in Treece's direction. His verse plays, for instance, though they were produced on the radio in BBC programmes, were not published.

His unique, romantic amalgam of image and story was to find its natural outlet in fiction. With hindsight one can see his novels outlined in his poems. It may be in the telescoped lines of the early 'Poem for Easter':

> 'The stiff lord
> Dangled from a fence, his thorny eye
> Shed peace, they say. The blustering tribal god
> Had other business on that day, alas!'‡

It may be in the vivid ballad scene of 'The Warrior Bards':

> 'So they came riding
> In red and in gold,
> With laughter and harping,
> Over the wold.
>
> No sword was among them,
> They fought with a song,

---

* *How I see Apocalypse*, p. 51.
† *Ibid.*, p. 61.   ‡ *38 Poems* (Fortune Press 1940), p. 23.

Safe in their kingdom,
The children of Spring.

Only their falcons
That watched from above
Knew the grey tokens
And heard the black hoof.

And so broke the battle.
I watched their gay dead
Ride the gaunt cattle
Back through the wood.'*

or, in a more mystic form in 'The Lost Ones', a poem written 'in dedication to all Celts and their culture':

'And standing on this shore I hear
The old songs and the ancient tongues
Curling and coiling back across the years,
Along the road made by the sun,
Patiently suffering through history;
I look down deep into the lifeless glass
And catch the fleeting shadow of a sail.'†

In most of his poems a scene or an episode evoke the poet's mood. Many have an openly narrative form—for instance, 'The Lost Land' (in *The Haunted Garden*, 1947) with its impressions of Romans fearful in the mists of Britain, or 'Princes of Twilight', a highly wrought picture of the chivalric Arthur, or the series of portraits in *The Exiles* (1952), which includes Dido, Electra, Jezebel, the old Ulysses, Caractacus and Hamlet (most of them characters Treece was to return to in fiction). Implicit stories, and stories of the past at that, are everywhere in Treece's poetry.

G. S. Fraser feels now that 'Treece perhaps had all the equipment to become a very good poet, but he never seemed

* *Invitation and Warning* (Faber, 1942) p. 37.
† *The Black Seasons* (Faber, 1945) p. 18.

to employ that essential gift of a great poet, the ability to "make a noise". ' Certainly in his poems he takes most often that attitude of the objective narrator which is the mark of the story-teller. It would be absurd, however, to suggest that his poetry was merely a rehearsal for the future; he was too good a poet for that. At the same time his dedicated practice in poetic techniques, particularly in the sonnets, was valuable discipline for the future, as he himself admitted. During the post-war years he was also writing short stories and though at this time his prose was decorated and slow-moving, he learned to organise his material into the necessary compact shape.

At this time Treece was also exploring the medium of the radio script and so developing a different sense of form; in plays and in scripts for schools' programmes he worked out treatments of Edward II, Tristram and Arthur, the Vikings and the Celts, and deepened his feeling for the past as well as his knowledge of historical fact. In the scripts which he wrote for schools in 1956 he combined straight explanation of event and dialogue that could establish character and atmosphere. The blend of fact and fiction so congenial to him was used again in 1962 in another schools' series on the Viking, Saxon and Norman invasions of Britain, and also in his information books.

In the scripts of 1956 we can see the difficulty which every writer of historical fiction must surmount. In order to realise William of Normandy or Eleanor of Aquitaine as a person Treece inserted short interludes of dramatic dialogue which do not merge well with the narrative and which have the awkward sound of colloquial modern English; it was by sheer hard work and experiment that he came to the authenticity of verbal exchange in his novels. His verse/prose play, *Footsteps in the Sea* (at present unpublished), is a blend of intense, even overwrought emotion and pointed comment, an interesting forerunner of the Viking stories. It had great success in its run at the Nottingham Playhouse in 1955, as did his earlier play on Edward II, *The Carnival King* : but the medium was one that was not to be popular for long. As a writer, he had to find more publishable forms.

For many reasons, then, Treece turned to fiction, as a vehicle for his thoughts. In 1952 *The Dark Island* was published, his first novel, for adults. No change in a writer's life is really clear-cut, although the trend towards fiction now seems implicit in everything Treece had written up to 1952. His reasons for turning to children's books were no doubt as various. The dedication of the first of them, *Legions of the Eagle* (1954), to a colleague at the Grammar School at Barton suggests that she may have supported him in the new venture as one more way of helping children to understand the past. There is no doubt that when Treece's literary agent, John Johnson, introduced him to Richard Hough, then an editor with the Bodley Head, both men encouraged Treece to explore this particular field. We can be sure of one important influence that led him to writing for the young. He believed that 'the creative writer must be an *entertainer* if he wishes to share his talent with others, and the obvious way of entertaining is by telling a story—one of the oldest crafts in the world.' He used anecdotes and story a good deal in his teaching and recalled one particular class for whom he was contracted by school tradition to tell a chapter of an adventure tale each week. It was likewise a family tradition that he told at least two stories to his children every evening, by order extempore and often containing 'certain situations and characters preordained by them.' It was just one more step to telling stories to the wider audience of book-readers.

The last years of Treece's life, after he had retired from teaching, were spent in Barton, where he enjoyed a busy and methodical working life in the day-to-day routine of a particularly united family. His relationship with his daughter Jenny and his son Richard was a very happy one. He watched with absorption as they developed tastes and talents of their own and seems to have been able to keep from interfering—no small achievement in a father who was teaching at the school where his daughter was a pupil.

The relaxed enjoyment of his children's company was extended to other children as well. In the last years of his life Treece was much in demand as a lecturer to the young. A strong dramatic sense, enthusiasm and knowledge combined to make his appearances memorable. Miss Esmé Green recalls one of Nottinghamshire's Book Fairs, held at Newark in the summer of 1962, when he addressed around a thousand children from secondary schools, between the ages of eleven and thirteen, on enjoying history in books:

'On this occasion he brought with him a sword, a stirrup and an earring which he used as a visual aid to make history in books come alive. Incidentally he carried these objects in a guitar case and the children really thought he was "with it".'*

It was at Lincoln during a Book Week that he tried a still more striking visual aid in collaboration with Ewart Oakeshott (who now uses the device often on similar occasions). The Director of Lincoln's City Library describes an occasion which thrilled the children:

'Their attention was built up by means of a fascinating story based on a historical background and at an appropriate moment Henry Treece withdrew a boxwood whistle from his pocket and called up a man in armour from the fifteenth century. He then proceeded to demonstrate the use of the

* Personal communication from Miss Esmé Green, 1969.

armour and commented on the design of the several parts of the suit to meet the requirements of the knight at the tournament.'*

His last lecture to children was on May 18, 1966, in an area of Lambeth Borough where the fine new children's library at South Island caters for children from poor homes and poor reading backgrounds. Janet Hill, Lambeth's children's librarian, remembers his performance as the most successful and impressive she has yet seen:

'He started off by telling the audience why he would like to have been a Viking, and what he thought their outstanding characteristics were . . . they were spellbound, because he spoke with great conviction and enthusiasm and a total lack of condescension; though it was more than that—it wasn't just that he treated them with great seriousness and courtesy. He was genuinely interested in what *they* said and thought, and what they expressed evoked a thoughtful response in him. I wish I could remember the questions. They went on for over an hour, and we stopped before they were exhausted. Some of them trivial, but many thoughtful, and he always developed them in his answer.

He was such a stimulating person to talk to, and in a way this was just an extension of a conversation he would have with one or two people—tossing out ideas and so on; and they all shared in it, and quite clearly had never met such a more-than-life-size character before. This was something I found tremendously moving. Their circle of acquaintances was probably limited, and almost certainly included no one like this. Afterwards the children left, and he stayed for tea. About half an hour later, as we were waiting in the hall for his taxi, one of the youngsters came in, having been home, on his way back upstairs to the library. As he shot past he nodded and said casually, "'Ullo, Mr Treece" as to an old

* Personal communication from Mr F. T. Baker, 1969.

18

acquaintance, and this was perhaps the nicest tribute.'*

Treece would never protect his working hours against children—and rarely against anyone, although as a writer he was bound to suffer from outside interruptions. Instead of ignoring pleas for help with a thesis or requests for personal reminiscences, he dealt with every letter he received, by return of post if he could, and always fully and conscientiously.

A writer of great energy and versatility, he liked to work on two or even three books concurrently. He often used a tape recorder to check the rhythm of his sentences, for he always felt he was 'telling' his stories. He had a scholar's attitude to fact and checked his material, in reference books, through personal discussion, in visits to places, until he was completely satisfied. Ideas came to him in profusion and were discussed fully with his editors, with whom he preserved a cheerful relationship. He relied on them to restrain his more exuberant plans, trusted their judgement in minutiae (though firm if after consideration he still felt he was right) and used them, as he used his agent John Johnson through his lifetime, as a sounding-board for his ideas. His letters to those who worked with him give an unusual and fascinating insight into his methods of work and the fertility of his mind. He was always ready to experiment. Not long before he died he was working on an opera based on his novel *Electra*; he was a pianist of concert standard and had an eclectic taste in music. In a life by some standards uneventful, Henry Treece added colour to his days by his great mental energy and his eagerness for new ideas, in books or in his friends. His death on June 10, 1966, brought tragically to an end the expression of a very full and rich personality.

* Personal communication from Miss Janet Hill, 1969.

II

Treece's books for children often have an adult counterpart with a fuller emotional treatment of his theme. His work groups itself naturally according to the periods which most strongly roused his imagination—Ancient Greece, Bronze Age and Roman Britain, the centuries of Viking activity. A chronological discussion of his work would cut across the natural grouping which shows so clearly the archetypal ideas on which his stories, no less than his poems, are based. It was not through paucity of material that he chose to use the same subject several times, though a researcher can hardly be blamed if he plays the thrifty housewife with his unused notes. Each time Treece wrote of ancient man, to take one example, he was experimenting with ways of relating the cycle of the seasons to man's birth and his passage towards death. The theme is strongly asserted in a fine adult novel, *The Golden Strangers* (1956) which describes the brave stand of an Iron Age tribe against invading Bronze Age cattlemen. In *Men of the Hills*, published in the following year, the story is modified for the young, with much of the irrational brutality left out and with two young boys placed in the fore-front of the action. Ten years and many books later the theme was to receive its deepest and most remarkable treatment in *The Dream-Time*. Books as closely related as these must necessarily be discussed together and it has seemed logical to use the framework of associated stories, rather than a strictly chronological scheme, for the present monograph.

Treece's first book for children has a complex genealogy. The recurrent patterns of life were always clearest to him

in the history of the Celtic races; it was the archetypal
pattern of the 'seeding, burgeoning, dying year' that he saw
reflected in the cycle of the Sown Man—'man's coming, his
delight in his full strength, and his going back into the
ground as manure.' Then, too, the conflict between order
and the artist's anarchy seemed to him to be enacted in a
way in the clash of Celt and Roman. In an early short story,
'I Cannot Go Hunting Tomorrow' (whose title he gave to
his collection of short stories published in 1946) he demonstrated the racial contrast in the amity between a Roman
captain and a Belgic chieftain who were forced into official
hostility. A few years later a short narrative poem, 'Caractacus,' enlarged the theme:

> 'No one had ever thought
> That Rome's far distant ear could listen through
> The cracks that summer had left in our walls.'*

The tragedy of Caractacus and his defeat by Aulus Plautius
was developed into a verse drama; this was broadcast three
times in the BBC's Third Programme. When Treece was
unsuccessful in finding a publisher for this play he reworked
its material in his first novel, *The Dark Island* (1952), as a
way of externalising his feelings. In its turn *The Dark Island*
formed the basis for his first story for children, *Legions of
the Eagle* (1954).

In this junior novel the schoolmaster has taken over
(though not by any means completely) from the poet.
Legions of the Eagle, published only two years after its
predecessor, is very close to it in plot, theme and documentation. Yet it is only in the opening chapter that the children's book comes anywhere near the ancient magic that
haunts the earlier one, when the two boys, Gwydion and
Math, show in halting words their terror at the killing of a

* *The Exiles* (Faber, 1952) p. 51.

hare, the totem animal of the tribe. The superstition and cruelty behind such beliefs did not seem in the 1950s (nor does it always seem now) to fit the kind of historical story designed for readers from nine or ten upwards, who are invited to identify themselves with a hero little older than they are.

Legions of the Eagle was planned to show the conflict between Roman *gravitas* and Celtic passion in its simplest form, because the conflict had to be within the emotional experience of boys, not of men. Historical stories are by their very nature didactic. But in his preamble to *Legions of the Eagle* (the 'About this book' which he almost always felt was necessary for his children's books) Treece gave the merest outline of the situation in A.D. 43. His true educational purpose, far nearer to story-telling than to classroom teaching, is contained in his penultimate paragraph:

'This is a story of battle and treachery, as might be expected where so many peoples were living together, each with its own kings and heroes and beliefs. But at the end you will see that the point the tale tries to make is that it doesn't matter what colour your hair is, or what language you speak. The important thing is—what sort of person are you?'*

It is significant that this book was originally called *Boy of the Belgae*. During the twelve years when Treece was writing for the young he grew gradually bolder and easier in his choice of material for them but he always considered their tastes, capacities and interests. As a teacher he knew how to bring the past to life *actively*, in scenes where period details would seem most natural. The accepted formula of the 1950s by which historical events were arranged round a young hero must have seemed to him congenial and con-

* *Legions of the Eagle* (Bodley Head, 1954) p. 8.

venient. For his first story, then, he created his typical Belgic boy, Gwydion, and gave him two comrades—a slave and friend Math the Silurian, an enemy turned friend, Gaius, son of a Roman centurion on active service in Britain. This particular grouping of characters allowed the teacher in Treece to range over a wide field of detail—domestic, historical, behavioural. It allowed the story-teller that geographical sweep which is one of the most recognisable points of any Treece novel; Gwydion's adventures take him from eastern Britain to Lyons and Brittany and back to southern England, in company with farmers, soldiers, princes, seamen and slaves. It allowed the historical philosopher to develop his thesis about the uselessness of war; Gwydion's Celtic mother advises him to 'take the oath to . . . Caesar and try to make a good, orderly world for men to live in'. Finally, it allowed Treece as a children's writer to enlarge the emotional understanding of his readers in a way that would not puzzle nor upset them; the boys in the story face danger and loss and forge their friendship in a way that belongs to boyhood as much as to history.

A young reader enjoys a young hero—so much seems axiomatic. The formula does not always suit the historical novel, however. For one thing, how far can anyone accurately relate the age of a boy today to that of a boy two thousand years ago? Gwydion is thirteen, his Roman friend slightly older. Their behaviour, as Treece describes it, is at times independent, at times childish. Occasionally words like 'cheeky' or 'thrilling' diminish their stature and suggest schoolboys of today in fancy-dress. In these early stories for children Treece was satisfying a reading public which has been educated over the years (and Treece himself has played his part here) to accept more sophisticated and more mature concepts of the people in history. The suggestion of play-

fulness in *Legions of the Eagle* inhibits a really strong
emotional tension and leads to an almost sentimental
ending.

There is a more practical difficulty also. The author has
to invent plausible ways of involving mere boys in events of
historical importance. This problem hardly arises in his
first story, since it is essentially about private and fictitious
characters. Gwydion's glimpses of Caractacus are brief and
distant, nor does the boy act in any way that would seem to
affect the course of known events. Treece's next story,
The Eagles Have Flown (1954), is another matter. This is a
chronicle of the year and a half during which fifteen-year-
old Festus is very close to that semi-historical figure,
Artorius, Count of Britain. The rationalisation of myth was
an essential part of Treece's approach to the distant past.
In *The Eagles Have Flown* he seeks to show (as Rosemary
Sutcliff, George Finkel and others have also done) that
the romanticised King Arthur of Malory and Tennyson was
probably a half-barbaric Celt who had adopted Roman
manners and military methods. This Arthurian story for
the young was a trial run for the fuller adult study, *The
Great Captains*, published two years later (1956). Treece
felt that the period around A.D. 490 illustrated the 'growing
pains of our own country', as he put it, and in fiction he
could isolate this last attempt to bring back Roman order to
a country threatened by invaders from the north and confused by internal differences.

The plot he devised for *The Eagles Have Flown* is based
on the parallel fortunes of a young hero and a warrior in his
prime, a fictitious character and a historic-legendary one.
Part Roman, part Celt, Festus stands on the threshold of
manhood and right from the opening of the story, when he
returns from a journey to find home sacked and family dead,

there is a robust, matter-of-fact acceptance of disaster
which is new in Treece's junior writing. All the same, some
goodwill is required of the reader if he is to accept the position of Festus, who witnesses the naming of Artos as succes-
sor to Ambrosius, the first meeting with his lifelong enemy
Medrodus, the 'sword in the stone' and Round Table incidents, the confrontation with the western kings and the
battles of Glein and Dubglass— and who, in the Epilogue of
twenty years after, sees his lord stabbed in a street ambush.
If he is not in the strictest sense 'true', Artos the Bear, King
Arthur, is an established figure of the past. In Treece's
story he is inevitably diminished by the fact that every event
must be seen through the eyes of a mere lad. For searching
and impressive speculation one must turn to the adult
novel, *The Great Captains*. *The Eagles Have Flown* is Festus's
book, the tale of a boy bewildered by war and seeking peace,
bereft of a home and seeking a father. It is a stirring adventure story, with a great circular sweep from Watling Street
to Lincoln, across the West and back by southern England
to the Weald of Kent; but all the time the action is extended
by the thoughts and feelings of the young traveller.

A personal tragedy, the early death of his first child,
deepened Treece's understanding of the importance of
kinship in the early societies he wrote about. In his stories
for the young the idea of a lost boy finding a father has a
poignancy that makes it far more than a narrative device.
When Gwydion's father is killed in the battle of Camulodunum in *Legions of the Eagle* he finds a second father
(literally, at the end of the book, an official 'godfather') in
the centurion Gracchus who, somewhat stiffly, stands for
security throughout the story. In *The Eagles Have Flown* the
role of Artos as father figure to Festus is indicated when,
having appointed the boy as his cup-bearer, the leader

watches over him as he sleeps, at a critical stage of their journey; later, when Artos becomes Artorius and assumes a more lofty status as national leader, his closest comrades, Kei and old Bedwyr (convincingly 'rationalised' from legend) are near the boy when he needs help.

The father-son relationship suits the trend of our time to choose aspects of the past that will seem relevant to the lives of young readers of the present. Treece responded very directly to this trend when he planned *War Dog* (1962) for those readers of the middle years (eight to ten, approximately) who needed to be led gently and gradually into the paths of history. Returning in 1961 to this first subject of his, the defiance and defeat of Caractacus, Treece told the story of a war-hound bred by the king's hound-keeper and taken into battle by the young warrior Gwyn, who drives the war-chariot of Caractacus. Gwyn is killed and the dog is near to death himself when he is rescued by a young Roman tribune to whom he transfers his loyalty. Bran provides the link between Gwyn the Celt and Marcus Titus the Roman, the focal point for varied scenes—journeys by sea and land, the attack on the fortress at Mai Dun, robbery, theft and attack by pirates—scenes which are instructive as well as exciting. The war dog occupies the same emotive position in the story as the boys do in the earlier books; he is, in effect, yet another lost boy seeking security. Treece has not altogether avoided the danger of using an animal in this way. Undoubtedly it was a way of catching the attention and sympathy of readers at an age to be more readily moved by the fate of an animal than of a human being; perhaps it is mainly adults who feel uneasy at moments when humanisation cannot be avoided. Certainly *War Dog* is not a sentimental book. Treece took pains to use a plain, hard style and to make scenes of battle and travel tough and practical.

This is without doubt the work of a historian, not a dog-lover.

When Treece was following a theme or an event through several books, he took a professional pride in finding a suitable form and style for each version. Three stories of Boudicca's rising show this clearly; they are, in order of date, *The Bronze Sword* (1965), *The Queen's Brooch* (1966), and *The Centurion* (1967); and to these must be added the earlier adult novel about Boudicca, *Red Queen, White Queen* (1958). The Iceni rising of A.D. 61 was a 'ghastly error of judgment on both sides'; it was from this point of view that Treece approached the event, now from the Celtic and now from the Roman point of view. There was one character who dominated all the books—the Queen herself. His magnificent study of her in *Red Queen, White Queen* was coloured by his reading of Robert Graves's *The White Goddess*, a book which he knew almost by heart. Boudicca as he saw her is a figure of power, at once sexual and maternal, which has been directed wholly towards war. There was not room for such depth of interpretation in the kind of historical story Treece wrote for the young. Perhaps, to put it another way, he chose to write mainly within the nine-to-thirteen reading range rather than for the middle 'teens because he almost always had an adult novel concurrently in progress in which his deepest feelings on the common theme could be expressed.

When he returned to the fate of Boudicca in *The Queen's Brooch* (a story very close in plot to *Red Queen, White Queen*) he drew her portrait in clear-cut outline. As in the adult novel, he plausibly involved a young Roman soldier in Boudicca's rising. Marcus Volusenus, a tribune of the Ninth Legion, is a provincial, born in Spain. Free from the prejudices of an orthodox Roman, he has a youthful curiosity which enables him to see the Queen's reasons for attacking the occupying forces and to feel the power of her personality even when he is most strongly aware of her cruelty. By stating rather than implying, by bringing his shades of grey a little nearer to black and white, Treece made the ambiguities of motive in his adult novel intelligible to the young.

He also tried to get into his story 'the magic and mystery of Britain, as a Roman would see it.'*

Marcus's first view of Boudicca stayed with him till her death:

'She was dressed like a man, with a wolfskin jacket and hide-breeches bound round with coloured thongs of braid. Her helmet hung on the saddle-horn and her thick hair flowed on to her shoulders as russet as a fox's pelt. Marcus noticed all the gold rings and bronze bracelets she wore, but what caught his eye most of all was the strange tattoo-mark in blue in the middle of her forehead. It was in the form of a watching eye. And on her cheeks were other streaks of blue, in lines, that gave her a very savage look.'†

A short time before Treece had drawn a still simpler portrait of the Queen in *The Bronze Sword*, a story written for Hamish Hamilton's Antelope series:

'She was not a pretty woman, being olive-skinned and squarely built, with a coarse black mane that curled about her shoulders like writhing snakes. But there was something about her that was queenly. It was not the gold at her throat and arms, or the red cloth and fox-furs wrapped about her body. Her queenship lay in the firm brown face streaked with white ash, and in the blue caste-spot, the Eye of Diana, painted in the middle of her broad forehead.'‡

* Letter to Richard Hough, January 27, 1966.
† *The Queen's Brooch* (Hamish Hamilton, 1966) p. 13.
‡ *The Bronze Sword* (Hamish Hamilton, 1965) pp. 37, 38.

Each portrait reflects the viewer—the first a boy, the second a seasoned Roman soldier.

The invitation to contribute to the Antelope series was a specific one, to introduce young readers (from a precocious six upwards) to an historical event in the space of a short story of around eight thousand words. The length almost prescribed a single, sharply visualised scene into which necessary (and only necessary) background must be properly integrated. The brevity of the form called for the kind of discipline Treece had learned as a writer of sonnets. His attitude may be guessed from a general comment he made on his approach to a story:

'I have to start with the lyric impulse, which then spreads outwards to create the book, much as a poem grows . . .'*

Not Ordinary Men—the original title he gave to *The Bronze Sword*—suggests the impulse behind the story: the moment when Roman and Celt discover liking in their enmity is its true centre. Though Treece had been known to say that he 'hated the Romans', he could enter into their desire for law and order as intuitively as he could understand the doomed courage of the Celts. The hero of *The Bronze Sword* is a Roman centurion retired from active service and enjoying the pension and farm granted to him by the state. Caught between rebellious Queen and vengeful Romans, for his farm lies near Camulodunum, Drucus Pollio is taken prisoner and condemned to death, but his sturdy courage saves his life; the young Celtic prince Lydd, his appointed executioner, cuts his bonds with a bronze sword; the sword is later in the day brought to Drucus by his slaves, who have found the prince dead after combat with a passing soldier. The emotional impact of the

* Letter to John Johnson, March 23, 1964.

story shines simply from simple, finely selected words.

Treece conceived *The Bronze Sword* in terms of a single episode into which he had packed—through image, description, nuance—everything that was needed to help young readers to follow event and feel emotion. His American publishers felt, however, that the book would better suit an older readership and he was asked to lengthen the book so that Drucus's earlier life and the end of the rebellion, and perhaps also the Celtic prince's background, could be included. He worked out a scheme which would not destroy the unity of the original story; it would be enclosed in a new beginning and end so that it would remain 'in its essential form as the sharp end of the pencil'. Nor was he prepared to expand the character of Lydd; whose brief appearance and death add to the poignancy of the story. He is, Treece said:

'one of those people who stray into a book and then go into the darkness, and leave behind them a sense of regret and of loss, quite out of proportion to the time they spend visible on the stage, as it were.'*

The additions he made were very neatly drawn from sentences, even phrases, in *The Bronze Sword*. Drucus's reverie about a cypress walk for the garden became a short scene; the old comrades recalled as he walked in the evening became real people with whom he celebrated his retirement before leaving the Legion; the slaves who appear briefly on the crucial day were given a background and a small sphere of action. In the new book Treece sent his hero south to offer his sword once more but in the cause of peace. Finding cities sacked and old comrades dead, he returns to rebuild his ruined villa and learns, with a strange feeling of

† Letter to Ann Elmo, January 22, 1966.

regret for the bold Queen, that the rising has been crushed and the Romans can continue their shaping of Britain for the future.

The Centurion, as the new story was called, is a masterly piece of joinery; it has become a story with an expressed message rather than an episode in which an idea is expressed indirectly in the meeting of two strangers. Here was a craftsman who could work to order without losing the force of his feeling.

The Windswept City (1967), one of the last stories he wrote, was another assignment of specific length, for Hamish Hamilton's Reindeer series. Treece had first planned to write for the same publisher a short factual account of the siege of Troy and had then decided on 'an account of some episode during the siege' with a fictional youth as centre. As he wrote the story took on colour and substance which directed it to a rather older reader. He imagined a slave boy from Thrace, twelve years old, wandering in and out of the citadel in the last days of Troy. Devoted to his mistress Helen, Asterius sees that 'her famous golden hair looked faded and dry, and her face thin and sharp'. His hero-worship of Hector is threatened when she tells him:

'. . . there is nothing in all this boasting and sword-clashing. All these heroes die. The sword takes them all. It will take Agamemnon even, one day.'*

Asterius listens to the soft voice of pale Cassandra prophesying disaster. He sees Achilles 'bend and slit the tendons behind Hector's feet, then thread leather thongs through them and tie them to the tailboard of his chariot.' He sees the Lion of Mycenae himself lurking outside the citadel,

* *The Windswept City* (Hamish Hamilton, 1967) p. 43.

with his 'arms and legs as shaggy as a wolf, his leaf-shaped bronze sword, his terrible long spear.' He sees the Wooden Horse approaching the walls—not a 'horse' but a siege-engine of grim aspect. This uncompromising picture comes through a boy who watches and overhears and half understands and is at last released from the burden of tragedy to seek more peaceful worlds. With this favourite formula of the release-ending, Treece made it possible for one child to read the story simply as an adventure with a happy ending and for another to see its full pathos and beauty. In this involving of a boy in great events Treece had come a long way from the wanderings of Gwydion in his first children's story.

III

Treece's journeys into the past took him most often to what he called the 'crossroads of history', the significant moments when cultures and races met. He was not so naïve, of course, as to think of historical change literally in terms of 'moments', but as a novelist he was prepared to imagine points in time when, as he put it, 'within the great exterior Movements of history, individuals of opposing sides meet and learn from one another, merge and come to terms'. This broad view of the past corresponded with his apprehension of the basic cycles of nature and man—spring and winter, growth and decay, birth and death. He saw the past in terms of human beings and chose representative men and women who would stand at one of the 'crossroads'—it might be where bronze met flint on the South Downs or 'Arthur at Mt Badon . . . the twilight of the Old Order and the incursion of the Saxons' or 'A.D. 900 Varangers v. Patzinaks' or the field of Hastings.

The word 'crossroads' suggests movement. Treece believed that 'from some unspecified "Dawn Time" to Hastings' the world saw a series of migrations governed by territorial drives, in which the racial mixtures of our time were gradually formed. By 1066, he felt, 'the migrations had finished and . . . England was at the beginning of a recognisably "modern" period . . . from that point onwards there would develop a unity of races and cultures in this country.'* Among these migrating groups the Vikings were pre-eminent; the very name means 'wanderer'. Between

* Letter to Jill Black, June 10, 1962.

the eighth and the eleventh centuries these Northmen, by conquest and by intermarriage, produced, as Treece put it, 'an immense Nordic oligarchy'; Hardrada, Magnus, Swein of Denmark, William of Normandy and others were all, as he said, 'vaguely related' and formed a pattern of power in the known world. It was in these centuries, especially, that Treece found subjects for historical novels. The impulse to adventure; a certain ironical, extrovert temper: the map of the known world; these three elements offered plots, characters and documentation all completely congenial.

His historical novels can be defined in two words— journeys and confrontations. The pattern is particularly clear in an early trilogy—*Viking's Dawn* (1955), *The Road to Miklagard* (1957) and *Viking's Sunset* (1960). In these books historical fact, in outline and in detail, supports the fictitious adventures of Harald Sigurdson, a boy of fifteen when he first boards a longship, a warrior of about forty when he dies far from his homeland. Harald's travels aptly illustrate Viking mobility. His first journey takes him from the fiords on a foray to Ireland (though in fact the voyage is abruptly ended on the west coast of Scotland); five years later he circles the Western World, with encounters in Ireland, Jebel Tarik, Miklagard and Kiev; after some years of farming and family life a quest for vengeance and the roving spirit of the Vikings takes him from Iceland to Greenland and so to Vinland. Most of Harald's adventures, fictitious though they are, are warranted in general terms by history and saga. Only in the last book does Treece depart from known fact. He felt that Iceland, Greenland and Vinland might well have been reached by the Norsemen before the usually accepted dates. 'I have a theory,' he wrote in the preface to *Viking's Sunset*, 'that recorded history, especially of the early voyages, often lags behind *actual* history.'* A writer of fiction may be allowed such guesses provided he makes it clear that he is guessing and, more important, provided he can make his fictions convincing.

If Treece compels our belief in these three Viking voyages, it is not because of their hero. The three stages of Harald's life are knit together in date but each book seems to be about a different person. There are none of the perceptible changes which would be expected if this were a trilogy depending on character. Harald is a useful link between stories which are, really, about Vikings in their ships. It is the voyaging that matters, whether its motive is a quest for living space, herring shoals, revenge or gold.

'Dane, Norseman, Swede, Finn, Icelander, Laplander, Russian, Goth'—the men in the longships are described by another Harald in Treece's unpublished play *Footsteps in the Sea*:

'We are *many* men, who have learned *to live together* minding our own affairs . . . We build our longships by the fiords and inlets, by our own effort, from our own savings . . . we man them with free men who would break out from a bitter North to see the colour of the outer world; and those free-men work together, pulling in time at the oar, under the guidance of another man whom they have elected as their leader . . . Each longship is a little wooden world, within the greater icebound world of the North. Each man, in each longship, works for himself by working for his fellows and his ship, for his world . . .'†

The simple code of loyalty demonstrated in Treece's stories is not unlike the equally simple code binding the cowboy of the traditional Western film—a genre which

---

* *Viking's Sunset* (Bodley Head, new ed. 1969) p. 9.
† *Footsteps in the Sea* (unpublished) Act 2, Scene 1.

Treece delighted in and hoped one day to try. Robbers, marauders, invaders the Vikings were and Treece does not try to hide this; but he sees also their courage and their group-loyalty and that impulse to explore the unknown which drove them as much as the desire for gain.

Viking's Dawn begins memorably with the young Harald and his father reaching old Thorn's village just when a new longship, ready for launching, is making up its crew. Thorkell Fairhair, the leader, roundly asserts his reason for sailing; it is 'to relieve the rest of the world of some of its surplus riches'; but the excitement of the gathering Vikings suggests another motive. Arguing about a name for the new ship, they finally decide on *Nameless*: 'though she may be nothing at her launching, she may prove to be something at her beaching when she returns. Then we will give her another name',* says Thorkell: those familiar with the Viking sense of doom will shudder with them at these bold words. But the sentiment applies to the men who sail in her, from massive Aun Doorback from Finland to Horic Lapplander, frail in body but with power over winds. *Nameless*, *Seeker*, *Long Snake*—the ships almost become characters, proving themselves, in the course of their journeyings, and the Vikings match the longships in their casual endurance.

The tales of Harald Sigurdson have a basically simple plan that makes them an ideal introduction for readers of nine or ten who have not read any Treece before. Though the three books are linked in plot, each one has a different atmosphere. *Viking's Dawn* is a straightforward young-hero adventure. Treece even releases this young hero from adult supervision by that fictional device more usually found in modern family stories; his father Sigurd is accidentally

* *Viking's Dawn* (Bodley Head, new ed. 1969) p. 40.

caught under the ship as she is launched and breaks his leg, thus leaving Harald free to grow up and satisfying those members of the war-band who still believe in a blood-launching. Harald is 'young' in our modern sense. The hard-bitten Vikings protect him, Thorkell acts as a father figure to him, when he is ill he receives gifts (one of these, a model of a ship carved in ivory, more appropriate to a junior family story). The young reader may easily identify himself with Harald throughout sea journeys and land skirmishes. He may also absorb information. Treece occasionally holds up the action for a snatch of explanation, introduces facts about the Viking way of life into the dialogue, even uses footnotes.

In *The Road to Miklagard* the expository tone has given place to an Arabian Nights richness of setting and character. Harald meets the fairy-tale Grummoch, 'the height of a man and a half and . . . as broad across the shoulders as three men standing together', a simple-minded giant who cheerfully joins the longship after the young warrior and his friends have relieved him of a considerable treasure; he is helped by the merchant Abu Mazur in his exotic palace at Jebel Tarik; he joins the Palace guard at Miklagard; he pays an enforced tribute to the squat King of the Marshland on the homeward journey up the Dnieper.

This continuously active narrative is more strongly controlled than the first book of the three. Conversations are more firmly worked into the plot; with a generous allowance of event (treasure-hunting in Ireland, a palace intrigue in Jebel Tarik, fire and plague in Miklagard, chases and portages in Russia) the final impression is of a compact and economical tale. Treece worked towards compression from the packed plushness of his poetry and the lengthy simplicities of his early novels and the laconic style he achieved can be traced most of all to his constant reading of the Norse and Icelandic sagas. Indeed, the beginning of *Viking's Sunset*, which completes the trilogy, recalls *Njal's Saga*, which Treece was some years later to arrange in a junior version. Outlawed Haakon Redeye, with his berserks, burns Harald's farm, wounds his sons and plunders the village which is under Harald's leadership; in return Harald vows to 'harry Haakon Redeye to the edge of the world.' The blood-feud governs the story until Haakon's longship is found wrecked off the Greenland coast; in the last half of the book the settlers are tempted further by their Innuit (or Eskimo) hosts' description of:

'... a great land of rivers and hills and much grass, and such creatures as they had never seen in the Northland, creatures with horns outside their heads and not in their mouths like the walrus ... '*

If the first two books of the trilogy read respectively like adventure and fairy tale, the third is in the spirit of the Sagas. The terse, compressed style of *Viking's Sunset* makes selected details of landscape and behaviour all the more telling. The peculiarly ironic tone of the Vikings, heard only in snatches of talk in the earlier books, now becomes dominant. At the end of the story Giant Grummoch and Thorgeif, alone in Vinland after Harald and the rest of the band have been killed by the Red Indians, speak for the Viking virtues as Treece saw them:

'Then, to cover their grief, they walked together, chanting an old feast-hall ditty from Jomsburg, about a man who put his arm round a bear in the darkness, thinking it was his sweetheart.

But before they reached the bright fires of the Beothuk encampment, they were silent again. For a while there

* *Viking's Sunset*, p. 61.

would be nothing worth the saying. They knew that well enough.'*

Treece's interest in Vinland was still strong when he was asked to write a biography of Lief Eiriksson. He decided there was not enough material for a factual history but fell in with the suggestion that he should do a retelling of the Icelandic sagas of *Eirik the Red* and *The Greenland Saga*, which together describe the discovery of America at the beginning of the eleventh century. In his composite saga-tale, *Vinland the Good* (1967), Treece took characters and events from the sagas but changed chronology here and there to make a compact story. Characters are introduced with the customary saga formula—'There was a man who . . .' —; men hide their feelings in irony and bravado; the obligations of law and kingship, the rival claims of Odin and the White Christ, affect their lives. This is no tale of fortunate adventure but a stark account of the Norse colonies in Greenland and the precarious hutments in Vinland which were so soon abandoned. A feeling of doom hangs over the men and women trying to establish orderly lives in a strange land; doomed, too, are their personal relationships in their terrible isolation from the old world. In this book, too, there are hints of that sinister female power which pervades, in particular, Treece's three adult novels of ancient Greece, *Jason* (1961), *Electra* (1963) and *Oedipus* (1964).

All these aspects of *Vinland the Good* contribute to its unity of mood. They also mark it as a book for older readers, for the very subtlety of its simplicity. It might be best for the average reader to visit North America with the young colonist John Andrews whose principles are sorely tested in the late seventeenth-century settlement of New Camden in

* *Ibid.*, p. 160.

Pennsylvania. *Red Settlement*, published in 1960 some years before *Vinland the Good*, *is* a straight adventure story, clear-cut in its issues and with a villain, the Puritan Twenty-man, who rouses hostility without ambiguity. The narrative ranges from New England to the Whitehall of Charles II, held together by Twentyman's plotting against young Andrews and by Andrews's fight for tolerance. Seeking to understand the Iroquois, he acts on a principle relevant to our own times. When he decides to accept membership of Grey Wolf's tribe, to escape the cruelty and hypocrisy of his fellow-colonists, he suggests a point which belongs no less to those Viking tales where violence brings only a short-term reward and the life of the hero is often darkened by tragedy.

IV

Human behaviour in a historical context—this is the way Treece approaches the past. He is at his most confident when he can go off at a tangent from textbook history—as he does in *Hounds of the King* (1955) or *Man with a Sword* (1962). In his search for a definition of the Northern temperament he used an extensive map:

'If these men live between the Atlas mountains and the volcanic rocks above Thingvellir, they are likely to be much the same sort of chaps, eating the same food, talking to the same gods and goddesses, sowing and reaping at much the same time (within four or five weeks).'*

During the last years of his life Treece was planning a major work of historical interpretation for the general reader, to be called possibly *The Northern Spirit* or *The Heart of the North*, in which, with the help of contemporary documents and academic histories and using every kind of illustrative technique, he could marshal once and for all his thoughts about the Northmen. For him the word Viking had two meanings. It stood for the longship voyagers of story: it stood also for a way of life which English Harold Godwinson and Hereward the Wake could illustrate as well as Norse-born Hardrada, and which was brought to an end by, or merged with, the successful Normans in the years following 1066.

An unpublished short story for children, *The Man on the Hill*,† shows how Treece usually interpreted this particular crossroad of history. The plot of the story is almost absurdly

---

* Letter to Antony Kamm, October 28, 1963.
† Expanded from a story first published in *Boys' Own Paper*.

implausible. Bersi Thordson, a Norse berserk serving Harold as a housecarle, escapes from the field of Hastings and assumes the disguise of a churl in a humble Saxon household; when his disguise is penetrated he eludes his pursuers and makes his way to London to seek the Norman King, whom he regards as a personal enemy. A scuffle outside the Abbey during William's coronation draws guards and nobles away; Bersi faces the Norman, intending to murder him, is emotionally convinced by his personality that the old world is dead—and performs the act of homage. It would not be easy to justify such a gloss on history if it were not for the obvious inner meaning of that final scene. The story is an allegory of reconciliation, as one world gives place to another; a long historical change has been telescoped to make a point, a point which Treece made again with increasing depth over a period of years in three of his children's books, in *Hounds of the King* (1955), *The Last of the Vikings* (1964) and *Man with a Sword* (1962). His intuition and curiosity were roused by worlds in decay rather than by the beginning of new worlds.

Always conscientious in checking the accuracy of facts, Treece would give himself the liberty of extending or re-arranging them when he felt it was necessary. He was, after all, a story-teller, driven by the compulsions of a creative writer. As a story-teller he assembled his ideas about the changes of the eleventh century round its major figures—Harold Godwinson, William of Normandy and, most of all, Harald Hardrada. 'There was no great Northern war-maker after him,' he wrote; 'he was literally the last of the Vikings.'[*] In Hardrada he personified the twin driving-forces of the Northman, his acceptance of doom and his will to survive.

* Letter to Antony Kamm, February 7, 1963.

Treece's first sketch of Hardrada goes back to his early years as a historical novelist. *Hounds of the King* reaches its first climax at Stamfordbridge. The natural movement of the book is towards Harold's death at Hastings, but so firmly does Hardrada stride upon the stage in the earlier Yorkshire battle that he distracts attention for the moment from Harold and from the official hero of the book, his housecarle Beornoth. Still, in this book at least, Hardrada is drawn as a formal historical figure. In *Man with a Sword*, written seven years later, he begins to take on substance as a person. He acts as a father figure to Hereward after the swordsman has been shockingly wounded, physically and mentally, by the Godwinsons. With Hardrada as leader, Hereward serves in the Varanger guard; Hardrada confides in him his ambition 'to rule the North'; when Hardrada dies at Stamfordbridge Hereward feels a whole world has died with him. While Hereward stands as a modified example of the complex berserk, Hardrada is, in this story, the saga hero. His first appearance makes this very clear:

'There was a man standing by a broken old stone wall, looking at him and nodding in a friendly fashion. He was a very big man, dressed in magnificent clothes. On his head was an iron helmet set with silver, clipping down under his jaws, a boar-head crest scowling from its peak. On his broad breast was battle-mesh of bronze and iron, every other link, and trimmed below in teeth. At neck and arm were gold bands. At waist, hand's breadth, was a war-belt spiked and studded with iron. His sword was almost the length of a man, his dagger half the width of that man's hand. His hair under his helmet down to his breast flared red as blood, its plait-ends wound with gold wire.

Such a man, his tall shield under his armpit, leaning, his legs crossed, his sword-tip in the snow, its pommel near his chin, his spear point rising like a pine-tree over his head, seemed a god.'*

Hardrada could hardly be left as a subsidiary character. With the material in Snorri Sturluson's Sagas of the Norse Kings, the *Heimskringla*, Treece planned to describe the hero's life between two battles—Stiklestad, from which he escaped as a boy of fifteen and Stamfordbridge, where he died at the age of fifty. It was to be an episodic tale with the stress on action and travel. At this stage of his plannings it seems that Treece was more deeply concerned with Hardrada's doings than with his character, but when it became evident that the saga material would make an un-wieldy book, the claim of personality asserted itself. Treece decided to build *The Last of the Vikings* (he had chosen the title at the beginning of his planning) round Hardrada's youth, following his fortunes only from his escape from Stiklestad to his arrival at Miklagard and assuming (for the saga presents the fifteen-year-old boy as though he were already a man) that it was during his stay with Jaroslav at Novgorod that the young warrior developed. Once more it was to be a study of a boy working towards maturity. Since the *Heimskringla* refers only briefly to this period of Hardrada's life, Treece was free to invent suitable episodes without altering historical fact or even the accepted 'folk-gossip', as he called it, in the saga. To give shape to the book he planned to begin it at Stamfordbridge and to use a flashback device so as to present Hardrada straight away as a personage in history and to give the extract from his adventures point and relevance. In its final form the book has a Prologue and Epilogue in which the battle of Stam-fordbridge is described and the vision of Hardrada's brother Olaf warning him of his death is sharply fulfilled as a firm

* *Man with a Sword* (Bodley Head, 1962) p. 39.

ending to the book. This device naturally leads to the recoll-ection of Hardrada's past life, since it was after Olaf's death at Stiklestad that the young princes had to flee from their enemies. It is, literally, a flash of thought—hardly enough to disturb a practical reader envisaging the press of battle but moving enough to remain in the memory until, in the Epilogue, the last Viking is killed. Besides, the first appear-ance of Olaf is repeated more than once through the story; the sense of doom runs like a second fugal subject beneath the bold optimism of Harald's adventures as a young man, for his thoughts constantly recur to his dead brother and mentor. The final form of *The Last of the Vikings* gave internal size to a book which is in fact very short. The power of the writing and the arrangement of the story force us to accept the dual time-scheme and to feel that we have wit-nessed Hardrada's whole life-span.

The Last of the Vikings reads like a fairy tale, for all its heroism. The clear, direct style is warmed by the exotic colour of scenes at Novgorod and on the banks of the Dnieper. The descriptions, selective as they are, have a vivid pictorial quality. The book is dominated by the mysterious Arsleif Summerbird, a man of the same stock as that nameless Pied Piper whose entrance lifts from mere nar-rative the pages of *The Children's Crusade* (1958). It is worth noting that one of the alternative titles Treece suggested for *The Last of the Vikings* was, in fact, *The Summerbird*.

Arsleif is many things. He takes over from Earl Ragnvald the role of the helper essential to all Treece's young heroes. He acts as mentor to the boy, helping him to fulfil his destiny as a great leader. But Treece thought of him also as an almost mystic character, not altogether human, with something of the migratory bird in the way he drifts into the story, and with a touch of the 'King who dies for his people' in the way he disappears; significantly, when he saves the life of Harald and his companions by offering himself as a hostage to the fierce Patzinaks, we are left to guess whether they mean to worship or to kill him. Harald is the hero of the book, but Arsleif is the key to its haunting atmosphere.

The original synopsis for *The Last of the Vikings* followed the saga chronologically in its details about Hardrada, including most of the intricate politics of his Norse kingdom. There is little of overtly human interest in his manoeuvres against Swein of Denmark, but the years Hardrada spent in the service of the Empress Zoe in Miklagard already had almost the shape of a novel, and Treece used this part of the saga as background for a hero-tale, *Swords from the North* (1967). Here he had to manipulate rather than invent. From hints in the saga he developed a bitter rivalry between Maniakis, the Empress's Greek general, and the incoming Viking. The two soldiers, who in the saga are quarrelsome companions in arms, in Treece's novel pursue each other in enmity in Crete, Sicily and Jerusalem, and many episodes in the saga are realigned to fit this narrative pattern. Treece also recast with great delicacy of feeling the episode of the kidnapping of Maria Anastasia from Miklagard. The almost poetic tone of this interlude is enhanced because Maria is subtly linked with legendary figures of forsaken princesses. After Hardrada has taken her from Miklagard, their parting on Naxos is deepened by references to Theseus and Ariadne, making these mythical figures seem like part of Maria's own world. Hardrada's tenderness towards the girl provides relief for the bluntness of his communication with enemy or friend. There is, in fact, little warrant in the saga for the near-brutality of his behaviour towards the Empress, from the moment when he

first enters her presence, looking round to see, he tells
her, 'what pretty things you have which we might want to
take back with us up the river to Kiev'. The bravado of the
Viking is pushed to its extreme in *Swords from the North*.
There is a strong link between this aspect of Hardrada and
Treece's portraits of Hereward, and of Amleth in his last
adult novel, *The Green Man;* they are all versions of that
manic temperament Treece tried so often to analyse, the
berserk.

He had always been fascinated by men who, as it were,
demonstrated death through performance—matadors, for
instance, or professional boxers—and the Viking with his
verbal challenges and his uncontrollable rages was another
human animal whose aggressive display might either avert
or accelerate conflict. Well aware of the peaceful and
constructive aspects of the Norseman's life, Treece was
inspired to describe him, rather, as a fighting man, neither
glorifying war nor ignoring the virtues it could reveal. It
was his purpose to describe the disease, not to offer a remedy
for it.

His view of the berserk was very much his own. He
firmly believed in the romantic/practical explanation of the
word berserk as 'bare sark'; to tear off the war-shirt was as
necessary a piece of berserk behaviour as the boasting or the
foaming at the mouth. Not for Treece the practical but non-
romantic scholar's translation of 'bear sark', which merely
described one of the Icelandic warrior's protective gar-
ments. There seems to have been a real compulsion in
Treece to face both his interest in the mood and technique
of war and his hope for peace in the ambiguity of the berserk nature. *Man with a Sword* may be seen as a portrait
of a berserk with many reasons for fighting. Hereward hires
out his sword—for instance, to defend the Empress Gun-

hilda's reputation in a formal combat; he wields it at Stamfordbridge in loyalty to Hardrada; again, he fights against
the Normans in the Ely marshes for a personal reward, the
restoration of his wife and son; and, as an old man, sailing
to Normandy to William's death-bed, he carries in a bundle
the sword which is now the only thing to mark him out as
'being different from a thousand other ragged wanderers'.
Treece's title gives us the clue to the centre of his story.

   This complex and compelling narrative has in it some of
Treece's finest descriptions of conflict, by weapon or by
word of mouth. Then, too, the scope of a long novel gave
the opportunity for some of his most finely evoked historical
landscapes:

'The Isle was hardly more than a great mound of solid
earth set among waving miles of rush and marshland. All
about it water lapped in ditches and channels. Huge flocks
of swamp birds lived there, and water-rats by the thousand.
At night, in the moonlight, thick grey mists lay heavily over
that deserted place. Stumps of rotting trees stood everywhere, relics of a time when forests grew there, now blackened and twisted wrecks, from which hung deep green mosses.
No man, unless thief or outlaw, would wish to live in such
a place. It was an island of sickening smells, of half-rotted
vegetation, of strange night-noises, and of despair.'*

But it is as a study of character that the book is most remarkable. With a few short chronicle entries as his starting
point and with some justifiable deductions, Treece has
built up in the round a man we can recognise as a universal
type but who at the same time stands firm in a particular
period of history.

   One of the most brilliantly contrived and most moving
scenes in the book occurs when Hereward, meeting a

* *Man with a Sword*, p. 103.

stranger in the Ely marshes at night, is filled with an in-
explicable sympathy for the man he does not recognise as
his pursuer, Norman William. It is a scene in a low key,
taut with emotion and carried through with controlled irony.
This crucial scene shows the communication between two
people opposed in their aims, of different nations but, as the
disguised William says, each with 'a Viking grandfather'.

Treece was always conscious that his sweep of geography
and history could set him a practical problem of language.
'I don't know how Alfred spoke to Guthrum the Dane',
he wrote, à propos of this same *Man with a Sword*, 'or how
Harold Godwinson took his oath to William in Normandy,
or how Paulinus spoke to the Northumbrians, or Griffin the
Welshman spoke to Gyrth Godwinson. But they did...'
Wherever he can he explains how his characters communicate with one another. In *Swords from the North*, for example,
the Seljuk Turk who befriends Harald speaks 'very good
camp Greek' and the Emir of Syracuse proves to be a
student of languages. In *The Golden One* (1961), a brother
and sister, half Greek and half Norse, when their fortunes
lead them from Byzantium to Persia and Russia, have time
and opportunity to learn the languages of their protectors.
But this is to see the matter only at its simplest.

The Golden One introduces an unusually wide range of
social and racial types. Even the minor characters are so
precisely drawn that it is easy to miss Treece's purpose in
stationing them along the road that brother and sister
have to travel. The theme of the book is tolerance, his
intention to suggest almost a world citizenship through
the encounters of Constantine and Theodora, to show that
much good lay in the beliefs of the alien Eastern peoples
they learned to understand. This rapid, exciting adventure
has other origins than the historical: Treece wrote about it:

'I want to show what it is like for two children to be caught up in the chaotic world of rebellion, invasion, pillaging, flight . . . and among folk of many different races and beliefs. This is an archetypal situation; children from Greece, Cyprus, Algeria, Hungary, Spain . . . will have known it *in our time* only too well. It is not often treated by writers, yet it is very real.'*

For Constantine and Theodora words led to understanding: elsewhere, they could lead to hostility. When words are lacking, gestures may serve instead—and how often Treece's characters express their moods and intentions through gesture and movement. We see them in the very act of confronration. Like the two wandering children, Hereward is an exile who must establish relations with the men he meets. In his talk with William, as they fish together, whatever language Treece supposes them to use, they are communicating at a deeper level, that level on which peace may be based rather than war.

This dramatic meeting of Hereward and William compels our belief because of the feeling behind it, but to bring together an invented character and one historically authentic and familiar is a hazardous undertaking. When Treece wrote *Hounds of the King* in 1955, with little experience as a historical novelist, he showed important events from the point of view of a fictional boy. As one of Harold's house-carles Beornoth is with reason put in direct contact with his lord, but it is less easy to believe that he is within earshot of Harold all through the battle at Stamfordbridge, that his war comrade Finn is the unknown man who, according to the sagas, speared the Viking heroically holding the bridge for Hardrada and, finally, that Beornoth should be one of the last to speak to Harold on the battlefield at

* Letter to Jill Black, November 30, 1960.

Hastings and should be found, barely alive, protecting his lord's dead body. After *Man with a Sword* seven years later, perhaps Treece's most brilliant merging of fact and fiction, he turned to pure fiction for further exploration of fighting men and, particularly, of the berserk.

Horned Helmet (1963) is the most direct, and the most controlled, of all Treece's statements on the father-son theme. 'In form, motivation, feeling, truth and language,' he wrote, 'it seems to be something I have been rehearsing for years, and have only now reached.'* Here once more is the child homeless and wandering, caught up in violent events, finding security in the end. But we never feel (as we felt with his early boy heroes) that Beorn is a child in twentieth-century terms: right from the start he is a boy in Iceland in 1015 or so. His defensive actions belong to youth but to a youth that has been hard and testing. His thoughts befit his years but they fit the Dark Ages too:

'A covey of gulls stood over the blackened carcass of a seal, like old men at a Council Gathering, shaking their red beaks at one another, as though they were passing judgment on some poor comrade. Beorn saw that there was a lame gull, who could only put one foot to the ground, and he thought that this must be the one this Council was trying. He wished he had a stick to chase them away before they passed judgment on the lame gull. Then he thought again, and knew that if he did chase them, or even go to the carcass to see if there was anything left to eat on it, the birds would flap above the shore with such a loud screaming that one of the villagers would be bound to come down and see what was happening. Then they would find him again, and give him to Glam.'†

Beorn's growth from boy to young warrior comes in part,

* Letter to Antony Kamm, June 6, 1962.
† *Horned Helmet* (Brockhampton, 1963) pp. 12-13.

ironically, through his responsibility for the 'father' who rescues him, Starkad the berserk, who is ruled by the violent moods of his kind. Throughout the story 'father' and 'son' are balanced, the one growing into sense, the other acquiring sense only as age saps his energies. In Starkad we see the berserk as an anachronism, a species which is becoming extinct by the eleventh century. Wounded and worn, he is housed by Alphege and his monks at Blanchland:

'The priest saw the sword in the sheepskin bundle, and the helmet that hung from Beorn's arm, and he said strangely, "Why cannot you rovers rest in peace? Why cannot you see that those days are done? For God's sake, boy, that was well enough when the world was a dark place, but these days we are mostly Christian and know what good and evil are. And yet, Mother save us, you *will* go ranting round the world with swords and helmets, as though there were still treasures to be won, and kingdoms to save".'*

Starkad remains proud of the ancient Celtic helmet which he had stolen from a burial mound, but Beorn, returning from years of service in Miklagard, tells the berserk that he has thrown sword and helmet into the sea on his homeward journey, for 'The Viking days are done'.

With the same theme, *Splintered Sword* (1965) has for hero the youth Runolf who, as it were, acts the berserk, though now in the 1090s that old world is almost forgotten. Runolf has left his Orkney home to escape a cruel foster-father but far more to seek a world where he may use the old sword which is, to him, the prime excuse for existence. A misfit in the organised world of the Normans, as Runolf travels from Orkney to Caithness, the Western Isles and across to Ireland, he loses everything he possesses—parents, friends, treasure, sword—till almost by accident he finds

* *Ibid.*, p.86.

52

what he really needs, the support of a sturdy Norman earl who can help him to fit into a sane, stable world. These two studies of the blindly courageous, uncontrolled berserk have a general application beyond the historical background into which Treece has fitted them.

Both books are intended for young readers—to give a tentative figure, eight to ten, as against the 'ten and very much upwards' of *Man with a Sword*. They are short books, their simple geographical plots built round a few events dramatically presented. Conversations are clipped and to the point, the laconic speech of the sagas helping to keep the action swift and easy to follow. Simple as the language is, it can express humour and pathos, defiance and deflating irony, and can open to the young those expanding areas of human feeling without which a story book is nothing more than a pastime.

In the 1960s Treece enthusiastically accepted a commission to recast *Njal's Saga* for the Bodley Head's series of Heroic Retellings. Of all the sagas it contained most of the ingredients of his stories—strong characters, a feud which proliferated in battles and lawsuits and ended in conflagration, pervasive irony, and that theme of the uselessness of violence which the behaviour of wise Njal continually stresses. A strong story like this seemed particularly well suited to the active reading years of ten to twelve if it could be pruned and simplified and given a superimposed unity of action. Of the two existing English versions, the one in Allen French's *Heroes of Iceland* (1905) and the translation by Magnus Magnusson and Hermann Palsson, published as a Penguin Classic in 1964, he chose to adapt the latter because of its plainer style. The saga fell naturally into three parts— first the feud of Gunnar of Hlidarend over a dowry which led to his death, then the entrance of Njal and his sons into the feud through the obligations of friendship and the burning of the family in their house at Bergthorsknoll; finally the search for revenge by Njal's son-in-law Kari and the eventual peaceful settlement of the feud. Listeners in the thirteenth century and afterwards would have accepted readily the long genealogies and the profusion of lawsuits which were, however, likely to be tedious and sometimes puzzling to young readers of today. Treece cut the genealogies drastically and kept of the lawsuits only the dramatic trial of Skarp-Hedin and his brothers which led to the Burning. He also compressed a lengthy parenthesis on the coming of Christianity to Iceland and the sub-plot of the womaniser Hrapp, to keep the story-line clear. His version of the saga, *The Burning of Njal* (1964), is a fine piece of rebuilding that loses nothing of the spirit of the original. Reshaping was certainly needed, but in moments of high drama—the quarrel between wicked Hallgerda and Njal's wife, Gunnar's dream of wolves, the death of Gunnar, Skarp-Hedin's defiance in the burning house—Treece saw that the stark, sharp narration and talk of the saga could not be bettered. In such scenes he follows the translation closely, adding an image here or a phrase there to point character or to round off an incident. The paradoxical elements of the Northern temperament were here. The aggressive exchange between enemies could hardly be better demonstrated than in this passage from the saga itself:

'Kol Egilsson said, "Let me get at Kolskegg. I have always said that we would be equally matched in a fight."

"We can soon find that out," said Kolskegg.

Kol lunged at him with a spear. Kolskegg had just killed someone, and had no time to raise his shield; the spear struck the outside of his thigh and went right through it. Kolskegg whirled round and leapt at him, swung at his thigh with the short-sword, and cut off Kol's leg.

"Did that one land or not?" asked Kolskegg.

"That's my reward for not having my shield," said Kol. He stood for a moment on one leg, looking down at the stump.

"You don't need to look," said Kolskegg. "It's just as you think—the leg is off."

Then Kol fell dead to the ground.'*

But it is in the heroic death of Njal and the reconciliation of Kari with his enemies that Treece found the confirmation of his own way of looking at the combative Vikings.

* *Njal's Saga* (Penguin Classics, 1964), pp. 148–9.

V

During the years when Treece was working out his interpretations of history he also wrote half a dozen contemporary thrillers. It was not so long a step in mood as it was in
date. His thrillers have a jocose, throw-away humour, a
combination of sense and impetuosity in moments of danger,
not far from Viking bravado. The behaviour of Treece's
contemporary heroes is also reminiscent of the stiff-upper-
lip men of Buchan's novels and the amiably facetious
Berry and Co, and perhaps there is also an echo of the 'piece-
of-cake' idiom of the service airman. Children who like
humour with their heroics must have welcomed Gordon
Stewart, hero of four out of the six books, when he made
his début, as they still welcome him. Intelligent but hasty,
capable of ill-temper and pomposity, often afraid and
often outclassed by his enemies, Stewart is no superman but
a fallible human being to be admired for his obstinacy and
envied for his last-ditch good luck.

Gordon Stewart and his comrades in arms, John Ferguson
(hero of *Desperate Journey*) and crack boxer Bill Frankland
(in *Hunter Hunted*), usefully cater for Treece's own tastes.
Avoiding brutality or sordidness, he can enjoy through
these heroes his appreciation of boxing technique or the
calibre of a weapon. These are men of grammar school
and university background with the multiple awareness of
their kind, ready to talk about archaeology and aeronautics,
the composition of a picture or the layout of an aerodrome.
The schoolmaster in Treece is present in his thrillers as
in his historical novels. He wrote as a man of wide interests

—and also as an observant father, finding details as readily from observing his daughter's taste in guitar music as he did from stopping the car to look at a Norman castle. The breadth of allusion in these yarns brings them within the range of Graham Greene 'entertainments'.

Simple in construction though elaborate in mystery, the six thrillers share with Treece's historical stories his successful travel formula. The first of them, *Desperate Journey* (1954), starts in classic escape vein. John Ferguson, recently demobbed and unwilling to settle down in his father's business, idly asks the advice of a London matchseller who replies without hesitation:

'Well, guv'nor . . . if I was a fine well-set-up young fellow like you, I think I'd get out on to the Great North Road and see what I could pick up there.'*

Jeffery Farnol could hardly have improved on this as an opening and, as with Farnol, the hero has worn little shoe-leather before he has found adventure—and is on the run to preserve a secret formula from pursuing crooks, through Gloucester and Ludlow to North Wales. The story is full of the type-specimens of its kind. The villain is identified as 'the man with the twisted mouth' and his gang include a huge, stupid bruiser inevitably called Tiny and a knife-man Carlos Montego, who speaks with punctilio; but there are minor characters (a vicar who has a knack with fire-arms, a cheerful Jamaican boxer) whose brief part in the story is enough to make them memorable. Each book has its eccentrics, its realistic detail, its well-mapped journey. In *Ask for King Billy* (1955) Gordon Stewart, as a newly-fledged private investigator, hastens north to Hull with a dangerous secret, by way of Brampton and 'Merton-on-Humber' (a favourite terrain easily recognised as Treece's home

* *Desperate Journey* (Faber, 1954) p. 18.

town). In *Don't Expect Any Mercy* (1958) Stewart is chased to Sark and in *Killer in Dark Glasses* (1965) to Spain and Gibraltar, to return to Lincolnshire in *Bang You're Dead* (1966); while Bill Frankland, the hunter hunted in the book of that title, runs down his enemy in Wales after diversions at Stratford-on-Avon and points west. Writing of places he knew, Treece could give real substance to his settings to compensate for the obvious artificiality of events. Sometimes incidents would be suggested by a particular place. A motor-tour in Spain supplied material for *Killer in Dark Glasses*—'The need for water north of Almeria, American interests in Southern Spain, the herds of goats, the Sierras, the bodegas, the Gibraltar apes. . .'—and helped to shape the plot. Indeed, family holidays in Spain produced too many ideas and some of them Treece had regretfully to discard—for instance, a scene in a bodega with:

' . . . a tense chase among the innumerable and mountainous casks of sherry, with the Cuban sniping at the heroes with a silenced automatic-pistol. Then, at the moment when Stewart seems cornered, Mike comes to the rescue by toppling down a cairn of empty barrels on to the crook, knocking him out.'*

The germ of *Bang You're Dead* (to be called *Northern Lights*) was a schoolboy's dream, once described to Treece, that 'the Head (who taught German) was an escaped Nazi, and a leader of a spy-ring' and Treece was full of exuberant suggestions about a villainous visiting Art Master who could be a 'Russian agent doing a survey of Early Warning systems in the north, or a double agent, or a link in a drug chain'.†
Clearly he enjoyed waking up clichés with a little frivolous exaggeration but he liked to be practical and pointed out

* Synopsis of *Killer in Dark Glasses*.
† Letter to Phyllis Hunt, April 14, 1964.

that 'an Art Master would have lots of excuses for visiting curious places—the dockside, the sailors' cafés, the ruined abbey of Thornton (where he might hide the stuff)'.*

Silencers, facial scars, secret formulas, fast cars—the currency of the spy story is used with infectious enthusiasm. The reader of today is apt to find a note of naiveté in these thrillers. Time has caught up with the characters and their light-hearted but basically single-minded attitude to their country's enemies: political ambiguities hardly trouble them. In their open innocence and unconfused sense of values the adventures of Gordon Stewart belong to the Buchan tradition and children reared on the Saint or Callan or any other ambivalent agent of the television screen might write Treece heroes off as laughably tame. They would miss at this rate a series of amusing adventures by proxy.

A master of the cliffhanger, Treece was always willing to experiment with new media. For example, he wrote *The Return of Robinson Crusoe* with radio serialisation in mind and worked out his story so that each episode ended with a bang or a question-mark. In the end this highly inventive tale made its first appearance as a strip-cartoon in the comic *Swift*. It was followed by the swashbuckling *Wickham and the Armada* and both stories were afterwards published in book form by the Hulton Press in 1958 and 1959. Frank Waters, then head of the Book Department of Hulton Press, was entranced by *Robinson Crusoe* and said 'it was rather like listening to a modern eminent composer writing in the manner of J. S. Bach'. Different as they are from the rest of Treece's historical stories—they belong frankly to the Gadzooks school—they still have the story-teller's drive behind them.

Treece could always hold his readers with the irresistible

* *Ibid.*

'And then...' There is one interesting exception. Apart from his secret service tales, *The Jet Beads* (1961) is the only story he wrote for the young with a contemporary setting (we may perhaps except the school-story *Merrick of Merryhill* which ran in *Swift* as a full-page strip during 1959), and it is his only book which is not dominated by the 'story'. There *is* a plot but it has direction rather than shape. The book is almost like an interrupted reflection on a theme—the theme of a boy waking up to life; Treece felt he had put 'a whole mythology of child belief' in the book. Bill Neasden is at a turning-point in his life. He is at sixes and sevens in his work for the Eleven Plus: his best friend may be moving to another town: he has an unorganised passion for drawing but no idea where it will lead him. A visit to the cinema and a chance meeting with a gipsy help him to an insight into himself and the world around him. The theme is too big to be contained in a short book for readers of eight or so, yet in an odd way it works in the story like a yeast, quickening the random detail of a few days in Bill's life—milk at break, a Viking sword in the museum, the sight of schoolboys enjoying an illicit cigarette, a quarrel with his sister, the tempting pages of a new notebook. Page by page the book offers acutely observed episodes, but as a whole it has a curiously tight feel, as though it had been conceived in a more mature vein and had been cut down in size for a particular purpose. Though there must be a good deal of autobiography in it, this contemporary story seems less personal than many of Treece's studies of people and problems in the past.

VI

Henry Treece once remarked that a certain educational assignment was 'as dry as carraway cake to a romantic' and there is no doubt that he felt happiest when he was 'telling a tale, getting things moving, getting folk talking'. However, it was inevitable that he should be invited to contribute to historical information series and equally inevitable that narrative should find its way into exposition. His earliest works of non-fiction, *The True Book about Castles* (1960) and *Castles and Kings* (1959), allowed him to follow his particular interest in people and places—and accessory dates and sequences of events are constantly enlivened by anecdotes and portraits. The *True Book*, indeed, begins roundly with fiction, with the description of a Celtic boy running from invading Cattlemen to the shelter of a broch. Only after the boy's safety is established does Treece explain the purpose and construction of the earliest hilltop fortresses and the change to the labyrinthal system. 'The past is all about us, if we have only the eyes to see it,' he told his young readers in a friendly preface; '. . . our castles are an important part of that past. Let us look at them more carefully in the future.'* His approach in these two books is that of a teacher *showing* something. Whether he is describing a castle or its lord, he wants his pupils, his readers, to see the past as a living entity.

In principle this is an admirable approach to a history book. In practice it can lead to over-simplification, particularly in a book which has to cover much ground in little

* *The True Book about Castles* (Muller, 1960) p. 10.

space and has to cater for average readers. In one chapter in the *True Book*, entitled 'Some people who lived in castles', Treece introduced 'dreary Bolingbroke', 'Richard the Fop', 'grim-faced William of Normandy' with little qualification. His prose is jocular, and exclamation-marks fly as thick as arrows in a battle. This was the only time in his writing life that he diluted his strong natural style to suit his readers:

'Actually, William came over in 1066 with a prefabricated wooden castle, its timbers framed and fitted together, and the great pins to fix them packed in barrels. It was not that wooden castles were the only thing the Normans knew . . . but the wooden castle was quickly erected, and in 1066 every minute counted!'*

Castles and Kings had the advantage of an older and wider readership; it is a much longer book and Treece took the opportunity to introduce out-of-the-way details and to use an openly narrative scheme. In each of the chapters accumulated facts about a particular castle—Tintagel, Ludlow, Berkeley, the Tower, Windsor Castle, Carisbrooke, Hopton —are worked into what could be called a romantic domestication of history. Here is no architectural explanation to speak of, no maps, few details of the way castles were used. The book is about people and their doings and although the later chapters do contain a continuous history from Edward II to Henry VII, they are instructive only in the most general sense, nor is that philosophy of history which dominates Treece's most simple tales anywhere to be found.

There was ample room for this philosophy in his massive compilation, *The Crusades* (1962), which led to a shorter book for children, *Know about the Crusades* (1963), in Blackie's non-fiction series. *The Crusades* is outside the scope of this monograph, as a book for the general reader, but

* *Ibid.*, pp. 27-28.

young readers for whom history has been brought to life in Treece's fiction may be glad at a later date to find more formal chapter and verse for his ideas of the past in its pages. Here, for example, is the pattern of mobility which led to the society of the Western world. Here are the cross-relationships which we have met in the crews of Harald Sigurdson's longships or in Harold Godwinson's army. In the chapter on Saladin, and elsewhere, Treece discusses the prejudice in some histories about the 'infidel' and summarises the essential qualities of the Moslem faith and the contribution of the East to medieval knowledge. In his preface he summarises his point of view:

'Both Christianity and Islam are Middle-Eastern religious creeds and, at this distance and perspective of time, seem to me of an almost equal worth. It is ironical that the conflict between the two creeds should have caused such a terrible waste of life, especially at a time when a majority of Europeans were still unconverted pagans.'*

By his sympathetic presentation of Moslem merchant, Emir scholar or physician, Treece makes the same point central to more than one of his stories.

In *The Crusades* there was no room of course, for fictional interruptions, but it is no less an *interpretation* than his stories are, in approach and in the points of emphasis which draw together chronological facts. Rich passages of description fuse action, actor and background. There is a fine account of Peter the Hermit's disastrous anticipation of the First Crusade and the fate of his band of humble folk in Hungary. Again, there is a short but telling description of the Children's Crusade, a doomed enterprise which Treece had already used in a touching story for children. It must be said that *The Children's Crusade* (1958 is hampered

* *The Crusades* (Bodley Head, 1962) p. xii.

from the start by its presentation as an adventure story in a young vein. The stark and brutal facts of this crusade could hardly be told without some softening, especially as Treece's central characters are a brother and sister who have run away from their sheltered château home in ignorance of the outside world. The icy wind of reality blows now and then on the narrative but we are always aware that there must be a happy ending for hero and heroine. Since historical evidence more or less ceases after the hapless children set sail from Marseilles, it was not difficult for Treece to invent a satisfactory future for Geoffrey and Alys in the civilised world of Outremer, but the ending, logical enough in terms of event, is emotionally out of key with the rest of the book.

Know about the Crusades, by contrast, has proportion and feeling, colour and accuracy. It is perhaps the warmest and most spontaneous of Treece's information books. Gone are the jocularities, the exclamations and the didactic parentheses of the earlier fact books. In something like ten thousand words he supplied an outline of the various major crusades, offered sensible and undogmatic portraits of the most important figures, and related the crusades to the pattern of the medieval world. From the strong opening sentences which set us fairly in the Mediterranean to the last rousing condemnation of feudalism, the book shows the mark of its author in every compact, forceful paragraph.

It was *Fighting Men* (1963) which gave Treece the perfect conditions for a major work in the field of non-fiction. With a generous age-range reaching well into the teens, he could aim at clarity and still match his subject with a rich vocabulary and a broad sweep of thought. To write a history of man as an aggressive animal he must call upon his historical knowledge, his power of imaginative recon-

struction and his practical interest in the mechanics of
fighting. Then, too, from the start he and his collaborator,
Ewart Oakeshott, worked with an intensity of purpose and
feeling that made misunderstanding almost impossible.
Treece greatly admired Oakeshott's *Archaeology of Weapons*
and the book, which he had used for previous work, to some
extent provided the impetus for *Fighting Men*. Again and
again Oakeshott would say in a drawing just what was needed to round off a piece of written exposition or to bridge
two incidents: again and again his background research
would supplement Treece's and suggest new lines of en-
quiry.

Treece planned and replanned to find the perfect form
for a history which would start 4,000 years ago with the
Sumerians and Egyptians and end with the Peace of Ryswick
in 1697, 'on the doorstep of Modernity'. Being most confident
with narrative, he finally evolved a plan for the book which
allowed a fictional beginning and end (a fugal shape, as he
called it). As the book opens a centurion and a standard-
bearer talk as they wait for the Celtic chariots to attack;
as the last chapter opens, Machiavelli discusses with a
Spanish captain and a German horse-soldier the advantage
of the Swiss pike in battle, the discussion broadening into
an actual account of the battle in question. In chapters on
chariots, heavy cavalry, the longbowman, pikes and muskets,
and on Roman and Viking warriors, anecdotes and quota-
tions break up the running historical exposition. There are
vivid and extremely practical descriptions of actual battles—
Taginae, Hastings, Bannockburn, Agincourt (with a masterly layout of the battle of Pinkie, a turning point in tactics,
contributed by Oakeshott for the end-papers). Everywhere
Treece tried to follow his prescription of showing 'what
the *people* were like' and 'how they went about their struggle

for existence'—to achieve a book which, though it may be used as a reference book, still seems like a story, to 'beguile rather than command and, by commanding, inhibit'.*

It was a tremendous work of selection and arrangement. In his anxiety not to lose the impetus of narrative Treece originally intended to use a flashback technique in the chapter on the Romans, starting with, perhaps, Hadrian's wall-building and 'letting a British chief and his son meet (a) a Greek freedman, (b) a Spanish Centurion, from whom they get the story of Rome, from one aspect or another . . . I mean, the skeletal framework: Kings, Republics, Empire—and dates of big men and battles'.† The problem, he said, was that of 'trying to fit an elephant into a matchbox'.‡ Reluctantly he decided that the plan would tax his readers too much and would be unduly complicated in a book which must make clear statements. In the end he solved the problem by commenting on the progress of the armies and letting the Roman concept 'feed in' where it naturally could. With graphs and plans, drafts and insertions, he fought each section of the book till he was satisfied that he had made his points properly.

He was not in fact as dependent on fictional technique as he feared. For the expository parts of *Fighting Men* he developed a style lucid, strong and flexible, for what seems almost a personal reliving of the past.

Fighting Men has an uncompromising subject. 'Man is a fighting animal, for all his words of peace,'§ we read in the Introduction, and Treece commented in a letter, 'Call it UNO, and it's still fighting—even in the highest interests!'.‖

* Letter to Antony Kamm, November 28, 1960.
† *Ibid.*, July 17, 1962.
‡ *Ibid.*, July 24, 1962.
§ *Fighting Men* (Brockhampton, 1963).
‖ Letter to Antony Kamm, November 26, 1962.

It was not always easy for his readers to notice his reservations about war in the full flush of a story but those who still believe he exalted war might change their minds after rereading his chapter on the Vikings—those hysterically heroic Vikings who made their own doom. He explains the particular scene he chose to open the book in frank terms:

'I used a small foray, because I believe that this was more typical. I also wanted to show an off-beat picture of a maimed Legion, not the full-scale triumphant one shown later in the book; because that, too, must often have been typical. I wanted to foreshadow the tragedy of fighting-men and not always show the big glory and the trumpets. This is implicit in all my writing—that I abhor violence, and distrust victory. I see war as something horrid and usually inglorious. When I use violence and victory and glory, they are often means to my end of illustrating that it doesn't *really* work out.'*

Undoubtedly one of Treece's qualifications for writing a book about war was his own experience of fighting, whether in the formal contest of boxing or in more drastic fields—and his capacity for seeing the reasons behind the choice of a weapon or a piece of strategy. An armed legionary could only put out his full strength for fifteen minutes; this dictated the particular way the Romans used foot-soldiers in battle. In the treeless Steppes bows were made not of wood but of layers of horn bound together, derived from sheep or cattle; the impact of arrows from these bows was different from that of bows made of yew, and tactics would vary accordingly. The success of the Viking as a pirate depended partly on the shallow draught of the longship, which could penetrate where no ship had ever been before. Again and again Treece gave his readers the

* *Ibid.*

67

relevant practical detail. Nor did he take anything on trust. To check the range and power of arrows he consulted Lincolnshire's County Champion and concluded that the 'great feats of the past, if done at all, were done by supreme and highly-gifted masters, and not by the rank and file'.* He was inclined to doubt that Viking warriors could catch a spear in full flight and return it against the thrower, as in story they often did. Could a man's return throw be so strong that the spear 'pierced the man and stood out beyond his back'? Would not the warrior be too much encumbered with sword and shield to catch a spear in time to return it? Common sense and reason, and still more, research, dictated Treece's final summary of possibilities:

'As spearmen, some Vikings were strong enough to cast their weapon right through their enemy, while some were keen-eyed enough to catch their opponent's spear in mid-flight and to throw it back again. At close quarters, however, the spear was used as a thrusting implement, and then the enemy tried to jump up and straddle it as it came for him. Otherwise, he caught its point in his shield and then wrestled to drag it out of the spearman's grasp.'†

Treece could be trusted not to glorify fighting and not to foist improbabilities on to readers who had the acute and deflating attitude of the young.

In the surreptitious revolution in the teaching of history in the present century Treece must be accorded a place. If his teaching of history (history within English, in his class-room days) was lit by excitement and a sense of drama, it was enriched by his knowledgeable common sense. A battle to him was not a date, a place and a result but a moment of human activity in extreme stress, when the most effective

* *Ibid.*, February 26, 1963.
† *Fighting Men*, p. 91.

arm-movement and the strongest emotion could exist simultaneously. In *The Bombard* (1959), a tale of Crecy and after, Treece used his knowledge of warfare brilliantly to describe the earliest cannon—how it was thought out, modified, constructed, used. His account of the reduction of a Welsh castle is a masterpiece of terse, concrete action-writing. But *The Bombard* has the ambivalence that is everywhere in *Fighting Men*, and indeed in all his work; to the end of his days he was a man who hated war but loved the brave warrior.

VII

It is sometimes assumed that an adult writer who turns to writing for children is descending—giving himself a rest, as it were, from loftier, harder work. Such a view is as insulting to a serious writer as it is to his young readers. After he turned from poetry to prose Treece wrote adult and junior stories concurrently with equal method and drive. His versatility never led him to relax his high standard of writing. He brought the same care to a short story for a seven-year-old as he did to a long mature novel; his search for the best possible style and form was equally determined. His early fiction, for whatever readership, showed the fault of super-fluity. He had to learn to discipline his delight in a pictorial past, to select from an overplus of material, to let action speak for itself instead of loading it with explanation. He had always tried to avoid a latinate, polysyllabic style but even so his early books show the indulgence of a man in love with words. Seven years of practice and experiment lie between the two passages quoted below:

'The moon was high, when they reached the ruined earth-works, and shone down eerily upon tumbled men and horses who lay here and there upon the ground, throwing a gentle silver light upon this sad carnage, picking out here a raised hand, there a broken helmet; throwing a malicious illumi-nation over things which seemed to cry out for secrecy and peace. High on the summit of the hill, the ruined fortress occasionally threw up a transient glow of light, as some last beam or stretch of thatch caught fire, and burned itself to an ember. The battle was over, and now across the broad and undulating field, men and even women were moving slowly, some of them carrying torches, seeking their dead, or tearing off the finery of those who were helpless to resist them.'*

'At first the fire moved slowly like a river of molten lead, nibbling at one house and then another, without haste. But all at once its nature changed; the great white-faced square mansions of the merchants and minor princes suddenly sprang into a violent life of flame, their high walls acting like chimneys to draw up the blaze. All over the northern area of the city such buildings flowered terribly and died down almost as quickly, burned-out shells. The wind continued until dawn, and by that time almost a third of the city was glowing like a charcoal brazier.

Avenues of dry cedars flared up, the flame running from tree to tree in one swift movement. The lead roofs of churches and chapels suddenly became liquid and cascaded down into the streets. So great was the heat coming from the Chapel of Justinian that the cobble-stones all about it went as white as chalk and exploded with sharp cracks.'†

Sharing the same flexible narrative technique, *Legions of the Eagle* and *The Golden One* are strikingly different in their impact. From an almost static picture we have moved to a strongly metaphorical yet concrete piece of writing which gives a feeling of immediacy and movement. *The Golden One* and *Man with a Sword* show at its best Treece's more extended, decorated, narrative style. Under the influence of the sagas he came more and more to believe that action should be the basis of his story and he worked to achieve a concise prose (foreshadowed in *Viking's Sunset*) in which every descriptive word, every spoken word should count. When he returned to the fuller type of narrative, as he did

* *Legions of the Eagle* (Bodley Head, 1954) pp. 96-7.
† *The Golden One* (Bodley Head, 1961) pp. 93-4.

in *Swords from the North*, he kept a tight rein on background detail and, above all, on his characters.

It would not be true to call Treece's characters 'types'—in any case the word as we tend to use it now has a derogatory sound; but they are not deeply analysed as individuals. Often they *represent* a stage in the development of a tribe or a movement. So tight is the bond between action and character in Treece's stories that we often have the illusion that people are developing radically when in fact it is their circumstances which are changing. Events drive Hereward towards old age: at the end he is still the same 'man with a sword'. We overhear the thoughts of Runolf, of Hardrada, of Theodora, but as they think aloud they are seen either in motion or in a state of arrested animation. We recognise them by their actions, often by their facial expressions, more often still by their speech.

This speech, however, is not idiosyncratic; it is essentially group-speech. Hero and villain, friend and enemy will use the typical Viking irony and understatement. They will use the colloquialisms, many of them dialectal, with which Treece often indicated the mood of an episode. In seeking words to put into the mouths of Roman centurion, Viking marauder, Norman soldier, which would not destroy the illusion of their existence, Treece ranged from the extremes of ceremonial address to the extremes of brutish utterance. In his first book for the young, Belgic boy and Roman lad talk as if they were extemporising in a History lesson: trial and error brought him to the purposive, racy talk in *Man with a Sword* and the savage shocks and vagaries of the language of communication in his adult novel, *The Green Man*. He struck with confidence the note of unreason, suggesting feigned lunacy in Amleth and emphasising the temporary madness of Hereward by a careful breaking up of syntax and a conscious waywardness of diction. As his characters speak we hear, sometimes, the thoughts they would not, or cannot, express.

How did the first men communicate with one another? In *The Inheritors* William Golding offered a striking example of thought becoming words. Treece's arrangement of words for human speech in *The Dream-Time* is part of a new dimension in his writing. In an early planning note he called this story 'Neolithic' but it is less tied by time or place than any of his other books. Literary conventions have been put aside; here is something new in the field of historical fiction, an imaginative form which fuses past and present, extracting the mind of the past, as it were, from a selection of archae-ologically justified detail, giving the young a major experi-ence of passion and compassion.

The Dream-Time (1967) was a natural stage in Treece's evolution. *The Golden Strangers* (1956) and *Men of the Hills* (1957) contain, for adults and young readers, substantially the same story of the confrontation of the Barley Folk, the dark Celtic race of Britain, and the invaders from the con-tinent of Europe, the cattle-men, the Beaker Folk. Treece deliberately telescoped the tribal movements of prehistory in order to sharpen the contrast between the 'dark' natives and the 'golden' invaders. The same tribes appear again in *The Dream-Time* (hillmen, the Hunters of the forest, the Fish villagers), the same life-pattern—the hunting of the wolf, barley sowing, festival gatherings for propitiation or rejoicing. Above all, here again is that instinctive feeling for primitive man which Rosemary Sutcliff praised in her introduction to *The Golden Strangers*:

'He had an intuitive feeling for what it must have been like to be a man in the time when awareness of one's own individuality—or possession of a human soul—was still

73

a comparatively new and a very frightening thing. He understood better than any other writer I have ever read, the
appalling intricacy of life in a primitive society.

... Stone Age world is a twilight world, with no clear
line, no line at all, between things spiritual and things
physical. And Henry Treece understood this, not only in
his mind, but in his very bones.'*

Treece's two early stories of prehistory contributed towards
the extraordinary richness of a book which is, technically,
almost impossibly simple: what is left out of *The Dream-
Time* is as valuable as what is put in.

Treece recognised two major social groups in the ancient
world, the war-band and the family—in its large sense of
tribal kinship. A battle is such an emphatic form of action
that it is easy to feel that Treece's pictures of the hier-
archies and training of men of war (in which he is second to
none) are his strongest contribution to the historical novel.
But the human relationships which spell life rather than
death were as deep a preoccupation with him. One basic
relationship, that link between brother and sister which
could be protective and could be anarchic, is central to
The Dream-Time. In his original draft of this story 'hero'
and 'heroine', if one may call them so, were lovers with a
baby from their union to bring hope for the future. The
plot was changed and, subtly, the relationship, so that
their love, while we feel it will change, is in the story a
brother and sister love in essence, although they are not in
fact related, and the baby, adopted when its true mother is
killed, is a symbol of their growing into responsibility. The
story becomes at once narrower and wider with the change.
We feel this is the world 'in the very early morning of
humanity', the world of a tribe in childhood extending

* *The Golden Strangers* (Hodder and Stoughton, Library of Great Historical
Novels, 1967), Preface.

experience outwards from the recognised physical world. Crookleg and the others measure counting in 'hands', time in 'breaths' or 'sleeps'. Encountering the Red Men, Crookleg thought they 'were so alike that they looked like one man many times over'. Treece chose the words he needed for narration or description, the words his characters speak, as though he were inventing them as he went along.

The vocabulary of *The Dream-Time* is small and monosyllabic because it must match in extent the patch of ground in which Crookleg's experiences take place, the concentrated circle of river, seaboard, forest cave, escarpment; yet these, as the monosyllables show us, represent a total world:

'So he went with her to the men's place and saw the hides being stretched and limed to make them soft, and the fresh fish being gutted and prepared for the hearth fire.

And in one place Twilight watched men over the great oak buckets sniffing at the barley beer as it fermented.

He said to the lady, "There are many things happening in the world these days, lady. One would not think that so much could go on at the same time."

She laughed and said, "I am hardly older than you are, but I know that life does not stay still".'*

Ostensibly *The Dream-Time* is a quest-story like many others in which Treece described the fortunes of an outcast, a wanderer, an exile. Crookleg cannot conform to the aggressive pattern of the Dog tribe; his thoughts and talents are bent on drawing and carving. Terrified of 'representation', which they have outlawed for generations, the Dog Folk reject him. He wanders from place to place, finding a comrade in Blackbird of the Fox people, he is attacked by the brutal Snake, the Fish leader, becomes the toy and protégé for a time of Wander of the River folk, justifies himself at

* *The Dream-Time* (Brockhampton, 1967) pp. 40-1.

75

last when he is allowed to see the secret cave of the Red Men with its magic-working wall paintings. Crookleg is a creator and a lover of peace. Fighting might interrupt or destroy his makings—clay figures, copper brooch, wall pictures— or the power to make at all. He cannot but hate violence and look for tolerance, the tolerance that comes from communication:

'He wanted all the tribe to understand one another. But when he said this to his father once, Thorn glared at him so fiercely that he knew he had said something bad.'*

Interpreting the book as a dream within a dream, we can almost see the tribes Crookleg encounters as the baser parts of his own nature which he must learn to relate to his creative instinct.

Treece's first synopsis for his neolithic story suggests that he was thinking in terms of another *Men of the Hills*. Crookleg was to be 'different' with his drawing but he was to be driven out because he was suspected of causing drought through his supposedly magic powers; he was to grow up, emotionally, when he was driven to kill to protect his own son. Superstition would have been the driving force of the story, as it is of the two earlier novels of prehistory. Instead, Treece wrote an allegory—wrote it in the first three days of February 1966 and altered it hardly at all afterwards. Using the past as an envelope for thought and feeling, he felt free to bring Crookleg in touch with races belonging to periods earlier or later than his own, to describe the artist in the very act of inventing the casting of metals, the glazing of pottery. To fit the spare shape of his story he wanted it to be produced as a continuous narrative, with no chapters—one in which the reader would have no

* *Ibid.*, p. 10.

interruptions to his emotional response. Conversations were to be virtually unpunctuated, the actual speech being denoted by italics ('It becomes more lithographic and plain', his notes said). These notes were not found until the book was in proof after his death but he had already discussed the question of continuous narrative long before.

In the printed book, many of the breaks in action or changes of scene are indicated by a small drawing—of a leaf, a hand, a fish, at once specific and symbolic—adapted by Charles Keeping from a composite sketch of Treece's, one of a set of drawings for the manuscript which Treece did for his own amusement and for the two children to whom the book is dedicated.

More than one of Treece's friends believed that if he had lived longer he would have written poetry again. In its emotional drive and visual clarity *The Dream-Time* has something Apocalyptic about it.

VIII

The wise writer is not surprised when his intentions are misunderstood. When Henry Treece began to write for children he had already made a reputation as a poet and was becoming known as an adult novelist, in which latter field he was quickly recognised as an important interpreter of the past. In the sphere of children's books recognition came more slowly. He suffered more than many writers from those anonymous dogmas about 'what children like' which as a rule, really mean 'what children ought to like'. With a curious lack of consistency critics would praise his power to bring the past to life while at the same time suggesting that he should have drawn a gentler picture of barbarous times. He was hailed as a 'modern Henty' but was blamed for writing stories of 'almost unmitigated savagery and brutality' and for an 'occasional tendency to dwell on brutality like a dog rolling in nastiness'. 'Even a juvenile reader,' one critic wrote in a review of *Viking's Dawn*, '. . . will recall with pleasure that every character . . . has been a long time dead.' *The Windswept City* was reviewed under the heading 'Brute facts for the little ones' and Naomi Mitchison (who cathartically shocked girls of my generation with her adult novel *The Corn King and the Spring Queen*), while allowing 'Very likely children have sufficient toughness and elasticity to take death and disaster and pain more steadfastly than adults can', still wondered whether *The Queen's Brooch* should really be read by children.

Over the years Treece's honesty of purpose made its impression and in recent years he has less often been accused

of indulging in a taste for horrors. A deep uneasiness seems
to have persisted, however, in regard to his themes. It is
natural that educationists, indeed anyone concerned with
the upbringing of the young, should look for books to give
them a sense of direction. A genuinely creative writer has
always to come to terms with this attitude in his own way.
Treece wrote about man the aggressor. In his interpretation
of the past—the serious interpretation of a good amateur
historian—the Romans fought for law and order in a spirit
not notably humane; the Vikings fought, often, for the sheer
love of fighting. Behind objections to scenes in his stories
which he regarded as 'honest blood-letting' lies the more
far-reaching criticism that he has no 'message' for children;
as one critic commented in regard to his Hereward, 'for
young readers a hero must be someone to admire and imitate'.
Treece's uncompromising view of the past did not suit, and
no doubt never will suit, the view that children's stories must
be not only harmless but also actively moral. Moreover, present-day liberal attitudes and concepts of international
affairs necessarily raise problems for the historical novelist.
In discussions at international level Rosemary Sutcliff has
been accused of glorifying war; the essential humanity of
her approach, her understanding of the components of
heroism, seem not enough to modify the pedagogic attitude
to children's books. So it has often been with Treece, who
wrote in the belief that children were capable of making
a sane and intelligent appraisal of scenes of conflict without
direct guidance. The writer, he felt:

'. . . must take a long hard cool look at his potential customers and at his own performance for them. He is not
patronising deprived second-class citizens or dumb pets.
He is not out merely to provide a drizzly afternoon's
soporific. His task is to tell his real readers about real life,

with honesty and respect both for them and for his medium.'*

Ignoring theories of what is or is not suitable for them, children continue to enjoy Treece's books for the battles and pursuits and duels in them. Innumerable letters came to Barton over the years, some in batches written in the classroom, others scrawled in pencil, a few from older children carefully typed. One boy sent a long appreciation of *The Burning of Njal* in which he assured the author that 'as I had read about half way I realised that all the blood-thirst seem to be coming naturally'. Another boy, who would certainly not agree to any censorship of his reading if his letter is any guide, pointed out that in *Hounds of the King* and *The Last of the Vikings* Treece:

'. . . included a rather inaccurate piece of information, in that when Harald Hardrada falls, mortally wounded with an arrow in his throat at the battle of Stamfordbridge, he utters some dying words to his friends grouped round him. Surely this would hardly be possible, as his vocal cords might be severed, his windpipe, or at any rate he would surely choke on his own blood.'

This forthright young critic ends his comment, "I shall not bore you with the rest of the gruesome details.' A class from a Cheshire village whose teacher had inspired an improvised Viking raid after reading *Horned Helmet* aloud, wrote letters that show how the action had linked itself with the characters who became real to the children as they listened. 'Lots of adventure and different things happening all the time'; the 'mysterious and adventurous' descent into the grave; 'the best part was where Gauk got his head chopped off"; 'I liked where they raided the village because it was very exciting, as well as having bravery in it'; 'ex-

* *'Writing for Children'*, opening talk at Waltham Forest Book Fair, Nov./ Dec. 1965; printed in brochure.

citing', 'exciting', 'exciting'. This particular batch of letters leaves no doubt about the response of the young to Treece's story-telling qualities, honest blood-letting and all. More remarkable, perhaps, is a group of letters written after Treece's death by children in a junior school at Pietermaritzburg who had been listening to *The Dream-Time* in class. Here are the expected comments on the exciting parts of the story, but also a much deeper appreciation of the mutual dependence of Blackbird and Crookleg and of the kindliness of the Red Man. Something of the feeling in the book had touched the children beyond the immediate impact of the action.

If Treece did not insert a 'message' for the young in his stories, he had something to say to them none the less. He knew they could enjoy stories in many ways and on many levels. He chose to *suggest* ideas to them in the emotional content and texture of his books. His illustrators responded variously to his mood but Charles Keeping and Faith Jaques perhaps best put into visual terms the play of feeling in his words.

His early books were well served by Christine Price's precise and skilful representation. She appreciated the scenic quality of Treece's writing but in the main did not evoke feeling so much as use her special talents to help the reader to appreciate historical period through visual detail. Walter Hodges's crowded scenes in *Castles and Kings* also gave an accurate and occasionally touching view of the past. The same approach can be detected in Roger Payne's drawings in *War Dog*, though he more directly depicts strong action as well as suggesting atmosphere. Treece always appreciated the care and vigour of William Stobbs's illustrations and this artist responded strongly to the heroic aspect of Treece's writing. His jacket for *Man with a Sword* interprets superbly the cutting edge of that story, and the exotic, dramatic quality of *The Golden One* is suggested in his portraits of Moorish Assassin, European Crusader and Tartar leader. Action is suggested again in Victor Ambrus's jackets for the Puffin editions of the three early Viking tales of Harald Sigurdson, and Treece's love of decorative detail is aptly echoed in the superb colour Wildsmith applied to the jacket of *The Queen's Brooch*. In complete contrast are the plain, simple and sometimes humorous drawings by Sillince which represent the modern scene in *The Jet Beads* and the equally plain, forceful drawings by Bernard Blatch in *The Burning of Njal*. Mary Russon's drawings for *The Bronze Sword* and *The Centurion* have a quality of intimacy allied to historical accuracy which seems especially suitable for stories which are meant to encourage younger readers to journey into the past. Treece particularly appreciated this artist's careful detail of buildings and weapons, in pictures that are as authoritative as they are attractive.

Keeping's drawings and cover paintings for *The Last of the Vikings*, *Horned Helmet*, and *Splintered Sword* are deeply interpretative. The jackets of these books at once suggest that the past is seen intuitively within. Keeping's strong sense of design gives a clue to the full meaning of a scene. In his drawing of the young Hardrada at Stiklestad the very attitude of defiance suggests the terror and dismay of a youth whose support has been suddenly taken away. The cruelty of Grim, Beorn's persecutor in *Horned Helmet*, is implicit in the stance of the man and, in contrast, Keeping has used a circular design for a drawing of the monk helping wounded Starkad which shows as forcefully as Treece's story does the inherent helplessness of the blustering berserk.

Faith Jaques and Keeping both gave Treece the feeling that he was in a creative partnership. Faith Jaques' drawings for *The Windswept City* are as stark and disturbing as

anything of Keeping's, though the minute detail and
hatching of her drawings are vastly different from his sweep
and spaciousness. Treece said that Faith Jaques had seen
'the angle-shot I make in the concept that lies *behind the
words*. That angle that a writer sees inside himself, but gives
up trying to tell to anyone outside . . .' This warm appreciation did not prevent him from making suggestions towards
a greater precision of detail and closeness to his intentions.
'Break Agamemnon's nose, please. A sideways sword-slash
would do that. His is too classical—though the rest of him
is good and right. The nasal of a Greek helmet only prevented the nose from being cut off—not smashed. Those
helmets were made of bendable bronze, not high-tensile
steel. I'm not being brutal here, but just a realist; he *would*
have a bent nose.

Troy on fire: Great—but I saw Hull on fire when the
Germans bombed the oil-tanks, and such smoke is continuous. A thick line on a wind-stream. No blobs; all she
has to do is put some continuous black in, then it is right.'*

Treece wanted the best for children and he was grateful
to his illustrators when they offered them as searching a
vision in line and colour as he offered them in words.

He was well aware that he was writing for a special readership. In choosing to divide his working time between adult
and junior books he accepted that to some extent he must
use two separate styles. In his adult novels he could call
upon associations and emotional experience in his readers.
He could expect them to respond to the overtones of his
description of Oedipus among the barons of Corinth and
to feel the almost appalling contrast between the physical
limitations of their city and their belief in their far-flung
power. He could ask for imaginative response to the moment
when Amleth, as King of the Woods, in *The Green Man*

* Letter to Richard Hough, May 7, 1966.

seems visibly and psychologically to *become* a tree. For children, the feeling behind a scene must be more explicit, just as the facts must be more clearly stated. An adult who knows Treece's mature novels can understand better what he was trying to do in his children's books. Equally, the child who knows his stories well is better equipped to get the best out of his adult novels in later years. The intensity of Treece's approach to the past in his adult novels had an enriching effect on his writing for children in his later years. Concessions might have to be made to youth but he would never allow these to be limiting:

'. . . I put all I've got into writing for children, and try to write at the top of my prose form. *They* know, the children, if you're doing a poor job, even if they can't put their criticism into academic terms.

Moreover, they are in our hands for good or bad, and if we want them to form a taste for good writing, we must see that their books are written by men who set out to write well, with no pulling of stylistic punches.

I work as hard in writing a page for a child to read as I would for an adult, perhaps harder. . . I believe children can take all a writer can give them—just as long as he uses the words they know; that's all!'

In the children's world Henry Treece will live on as a story-teller. The story-teller establishes an identity with his subject and with his audience. Treece wrote (of one of his adult books) that Jason was 'more actual to me than Queen Anne', and again 'I *know* about Jason—in the way that a poet knows about things, because he is part of them.' Children of many ages and abilities enjoy his books because he knew children as well as he knew the people of the past.

Notes on Perception and Vision

BY HENRY TREECE

The notes that follow were written by Henry Treece at various times over a fortnight as the basis for a lecture which he gave at the Regional College of Art, Hull, on June 1, 1966, about a week before his death. Together they represent the last and probably the fullest personal account of his philosophy as a novelist.

Treece was a very careful writer, who dated every scrap of manuscript. By no means all the passages that he wrote for his lecture were actually incorporated in the script he took with him to Hull and from which he delivered that lecture. Antony Kamm has selected in their entirety passages from the notes and from the lecture which seem to be particularly relevant to this monograph, and they are presented here, from Treece's own manuscript, in the order in which they occurred to him and in which they were written down.

MAY 17, 1966

To explain perception in writing is to attempt the ineffable. One's vision is more than the words on the page, more even than the images described. One's writing sometimes exists in its own right, apart from the print, even apart from the images and characters and speech. One can close the eyes and *sense it*—not as words and pictures, but as a unity in the mind, with kinetic quality and mass. A scene from a book, even a whole book, can be so felt in the mind, as though it had tactile and sonic qualities. As though it were rough as granite, or smooth as a pebble; loud as a drum or soft as an insect moving across a leaf.

Only when I get this three-dimensional feeling coming off a piece of writing do I feel that I have truly created, brought into being what had not been there before, (or rediscovered something that had been there once, but had got itself hidden).

The act of writing a novel is, for me, the slow, and lonely, and infinitely tiring process of finding how to make magic happen. One can learn it up to a point but, once this learning reaches a certain stage one becomes automatic, a conjuror, and the thing one creates lacks organic life. It lies stark on the page, has no warmth, no dimension, no capability of moving me, when I think about it again.

If writing creatively were simply a matter of acquiring an enormous vocabulary, and of learning grammar, syntax and the parts of speech, any intelligent person, with time to spare, could become a writer—a poet or a novelist.

To be, say, a critic, requires that one should be a grammarian, a scientist, a mathematician. But to be the writer of a novel requires one to have perhaps another set of qualities —or the same qualities in other admixtures—and certainly to have an extra sense *beyond* and out in space, in orbit, perhaps never coming fully to rest.

For certain sorts of writing are out in orbit monstrous, in the sense that one must be obsessed beyond normality even to set the words and the concepts on to the page. One must be dedicated, called, driven, by one's peculiar god, by the creation of one's curious magic. But this art is not entirely conscious, nor is the language in which it is expressed. The driven creator goes into action almost like a man under drugs or hypnosis, using words as they present themselves to give form to the world that is revealing itself to his inner-eye. Later, in cold blood, if he has learned his trade through the earlier stages of linguistic competence, he will find that the words, in the main, came to him right. The right words: the right sentences: the right paragraphs.

What then is this *monstrous quality* that has such power to drive the writer into his act of creation? What is *the force* which makes him sit down before five hundred virgin sheets of paper, knowing that once he has started, and this white anonymous mass has stirred into life, he must live with the growing incubus for perhaps two years?

Obviously, he is telling a story of some sort, and this will sustain him, will hold his mind together: obviously in his book there will be people who talk and perform characteristic actions. These too will help to keep the novelist going —he may even get his amusement, his personal and private kicks, out of letting these people look and talk and act outrageously. From such mechanisms, the novelist may gain relief in the bearing of his load.

But if a novel were only a story and a group of variously interesting people, acting entertainingly—*that would hardly be enough*, even though the narrative and its human units conveyed in the end a message, a moral, a philosophic answer to some dilemma posed by the book's theme. Such a book would hardly compensate the author, in the deepest sense, for the deprivations he had suffered in giving up two years of his life bringing it into being.

What then is the monstrous force that drives him forward, compensates him—and exhausts him at the same time? What is this frightful orgasm to which he submits, again and again, hating its requirements, but unable to reject them?

I see the creative writer on two levels at least. In one of his functions he is the crippled god—the maker who in his non-literary life is, or feels himself to be, somehow incomplete, inadequate. Yet, being a creator, he has pride, and a stubborn (if despairing) courage: so, he writes for himself a world in which the blind man sees all, and the cripple leaps over mountains.

On another more important of his levels, the creative writer is not the lame god, but the integrated observant man, man using all his senses and his sense, to understand and to set down archetypal patterns. Now this man will have only one essential tale to tell: and it will be the story of the seasons in their progression through the year—from the Sun's first awakening after Winter, to the burning of the stubble after the harvest. His vision will be directed to this ritual—dance of the months, the crops, the heroes; to their coming, their fruition and their death.

It is a primitive pattern, but it contains everything—the gentle colours of primroses and the sound of roaring thunder. It is a pattern over which a greater god (or goddess) than the writer, presides, and is acknowledged by him: and once this writer—who is the messenger of the god—has perceived this pattern, has surrendered himself to this vision—then he will know, without doubt, that all years are one year, all pleasures one pleasure, all disasters trivial, and all heroes expendable.

MAY 17, 1966

It is next to impossible for the writer to see an object objectively—that is, showing it for what it is to the camera-eye and for nothing else. A writer must use words and these words attract themselves to his mind and hand because of his part personality. When he uses them, he expresses his personality perforce. He sees a white stone column in the desert: if he says that, that is as far as he dare go towards an absolute.

If he says that the colour or material or shape of the column reminds him of anything, so much does he depart from the column and reveal himself.

Now the nature of creative man is to invest each object

seen with his full sense of it, his perception, his impression, his vision. And the more the writer allows his sensing mechanism to work, the less column we get and the more autobiography.

So, in the end, the writer with the richest and most diverse senses (and the least control on his surgical knife) will not expose that column, but will hide it. Not recreate it, but destroy it. That is the dilemma, the dichotomy, as I see it.

Perception is essential if writing is to have bite, freshness, individuality: yet, as the balance sinks under the cumulative comparisons, likenesses, relationships to the allied world of that column, so does perception smother itself.

Or, to put it another way: perceptions must be so inhibited, if the column is to emerge as anything like a column, that almost before he starts work the writer must prepare himself to put on blinkers. That is, as his pen touches the paper, he must already be prepared to withdraw (if he is to write of the column and not of himself-as-column). Consequently, the original first-sight glimpse of that column, the innocent view, is only remotely likely to come through since, close behind this view, is a secondary one which must be limited and even withdrawn to give the column a chance to declare itself: and awareness of what is already in store may tend to throw forward the writer's self-known necessity to prune, so that even the first words come under the knife.

MAY 18, 1966

Perception is the act, or state, of knowing the nature of anything through the senses, but in such a deep, sensitive, sympathetic way that this thing takes on an extra dimension and becomes for a while at least more than it had been before.

When the writer is so attuned that he can relate a number of such supra-things into a cosmology, or imaginative system, so as to form an entire and self-sufficient environment for his writing—that is his vision. But it is more than mere dream and imagination: it is such a co-ordinated pattern that, once it is explained, other human creatures can also move in it, if they too are in tune. Or, if they cannot actually share it, they can respect it as being valid for someone whose processes are not of their own sort. Sometimes the writer, catering for this divergence, writes closely alongside the thing so as to share it with others, perceiving the inner nature of the thing now in a related but more generalised term, and this we call a symbol. This, too, is his vision.

MAY 20, 1966

There is another point I would like to grope towards: it is this, that perception and vision in a writer—a prose-writer at least—do not operate 24 hours a day. For much of the day they are switched-off, and the writer is a very ordinary moron, moving about rather blindly, unaware of significances, just another animal eating and drinking and enjoying the sun—when there is any.

But there are times in that careless day when his perceptions suddenly go into action and his total vision accrues something more towards its completeness. These times are when the outside touches the writer's basic and personal theme—that central thesis of his life which makes him slightly different from other writers. I think that every writer, at some time or other in his evolution towards maturity, finds himself a thesis or theme (or has it found for him by outside circumstances). Often, he is not conscious of this and realises it, or wakes up to it, only a long time after it has been in operation in his work. Then he suddenly understands that he has been writing one book, all the time. Or has been rehearsing various versions of one book, unconsciously directed towards a perfection of his statement.

I was first made dimly aware of this about twenty-five years ago when, in an article in *Horizon*, Stephen Spender, writing about an exhibition of the work of Cecil Collins, the painter, said: 'Like Treece, Collins is obsessed by the concept of the Sacred Fool.'

Looking back, I think he was right at that time—though one's hard-core theme twists and turns and takes on accretions as the years go on. And, only very recently, I became sharply aware that for the past fifteen years or so the two principal themes in my writing had been the Father seeking the Son (or the Son the Father) *and* the theme of the Distracted Woman, the woman drawn away from gentleness and mercy into other, perhaps more sinister paths; the Maenad, the Bacchante.

I do not know (and do not wish to enquire) why these themes should now lie at the deep heart of my work. But what I do know is that my perceptions of the outer world, and the cohesion of those perceptions in my head (which form my vision and life) are directed towards developing and making clear in words—where one can ever clear—these two obsessive and compulsive themes.

Out of one's struggle to set down such themes grows one's personal manner of writing—one's *style* as it is called. Buffon said, 'Le style, c'est l'homme même.' Style is the man himself—that is, the man trying to record his struggle to make clear his essential and obsessive theme, the theory which makes him tick.

Yet there is a strong case for believing that the writer outgrows his own style as his vision develops. Looking back, the writer is dissatisfied with what he said, not because it was bad *in its day*, but because if he did it now, he would do it differently—because his perception has developed and the old words no longer represent his present development or change.

The writer is probably fighting a losing battle all his life, for his perception is perhaps always one jump ahead of his technique, his ability to set down the inner turmoil and its resolution.

MAY 26, 1966

There are some things that a writer senses or observes objectively—that is, as objects outside himself, and equally available to all, and having a roughly equal shape, dimension and nature for all.

There are other things that a writer senses subjectively. That is, as an extension of himself, he being the subject. It is as though he takes such things within himself as part of his own organic functioning. When later he externalises his subjectively-perceived images, it is possible that others may not recognise the original object of sensing, since their own perceptions may be of a different sort or quality, the parallels they draw of a different dimension.

In effect I am saying that the subjective writer is much like the oyster which takes in the irritant grain of sand and round it, for his own reasons and in his own dark and special ways, coats this sharp grain and converts it to a pearl, of whatever size, quality and colour.

If a writer says: 'A poorly-dressed old man came in and sat, half-blind, at the oak table near the fire. After a time he began to scratch at the table top.'—this is objective writing. But writing subjectively, he might say: 'He stumbled in from outside, from nowhere, crook-backed as a hawthorn on which dirty scraps of rag fluttered, blown by a long-dead wind. Like a moving tree seeking companionship of other wood, he sat at the oak table. The dry thorns of his fingers travelled across the golden grain, envying its smoothness, its youth—its prosperity, trying to wound it. Withered thorn against young oak. "Take care," said the fingers, "be you not proud. The little fire that purrs in its iron cage will eat us both in time. Then, of our mingled ashes, who shall say: this was an oak tree, this was a thorn?" '

I am not trying to say that the second is better than the first—or that either is good: I am pointing out a difference in the two statements. What the first writer says would be observed by all who saw the old man come into the room. What the second writer says has an extra dimension which depends on the writer having recognised a similarity between the old man and a thorn-tree. All that follows, after this initial recognition, this simile or parallel, leans towards an almost mythic moral—that we must all die and be equal in death.

This is the *vision* which grows out of the writer's *perception* of the old man. It may not be true for anyone else who sees the old man, but it is valid for the writer: it is a part of the cosmos, the regulated complex of impressions which goes to make his world different from that of the man standing next to him.

Or, to put it another way, a number of writers, seeing the old man come in, might each be struck by his similarity to a thorn-tree—but having done that, each would develop this recognition differently, according to his own personal temperament, experience, background: each would create his own myth, his own ultimate vision of the subjective world of which the old man had become a part.

MAY 28, 1966

Sometimes I feel the need to put sunlight, and dried earth
or sand, or vegetation, or salt water into my books because
I often write about Greece and the Mediterranean. I feel
the need for these elements not merely as background to
the human characters, but almost as characters themselves.
Often the scene seems to induce action or thought or feeling
in the people of that scene.

As a writer of this sort of thing I tend to push my perception to its limits. I not only want to feel the sun's heat
but to smell it—to smell what it does to rocks and flowers and
water. Just as I feel the need to *see* heat coming off a rock
or a man's face or a girl's hair.

This is not the surrealist dislocation of the senses: it is
something deep at the core of a tradition. Sometimes I
get so carried away by this that I go into a sort of trance of
absorption in which I am *part* of the scene, the sun on rock,
the rock suffering sun or frost, the leaf suffering rain, the
boughs in the wind, and the wind itself. Sometimes my
prose *is* the wind beating at boughs, or blowing blind over
empty spaces.

When my writing turns into this, it does not, can not,
tell a story; cannot push the narrative or characterisation on;
it is just itself then. It *says* nothing, it just *is*.

Often editors—and especially American editors—try to
cut these bits out, and sometimes they succeed if I am too
tired to fight them. But I would rather have them in—
because such fugal passages, such flights, occur only too
rarely in a story—and more rarely still as one grows older.

They are not flights of unfundamental lyricism, not *pure*
poetry: they are part of the organic movement of the piece,
of the story: without them the story loses a dimension, a
limit, is partly emasculated.

To an objective editor these passages seem to have no relevance: to a writer who *feels* with his body as well as his emotions (and even with his mind, his intelligence), they are essential—in that they are the *essence*, the Being, of what he feels he needs to put down at that sparking-off point of his book.

Such writing is not cerebral, not easy, not dependent on sheer thought. It comes from low down out of the pit of the stomach and the pit of life's experience. And when it comes, the writer *knows* he has to put it down, or he is being false to his book, to his being, to his talent. This is the deep part of his creation, his fusion of perceptions: this is what his vision *is*. This is what makes him tick, what his story is about, and what he is about.

Any trained literate can write a story, a novel of sheer action: but to achieve more than that needs the writer to be a poet, a recording sensitive, willing to be obedient, to put himself into the condition of the static stone, or the sea shore pebble, and to let the sun's heat and the salt tide's fury play on him—even destroy him.

In medicine there is what is called a Sympathetic Pain, or a Referred Pain. I mention this because it is in line with my own psycho-physical concept of perception in writing.

If you have a Sympathetic or Referred Pain, it means that the limb, or the tooth, in which you feel the pain is not the one which is suffering dis-ease (or disease), but that it is twanging in sympathy to that one; or is receiving pain *referred*, or sent on, by that one.

It is my contention that this 'formula' applies to all we do, in that elevated column we call our body. That a pain in my right arm might be referred from my left leg: or that if I run a thorn into my little finger I shall feel the pain in my neck. Or that if I *see* the sun, I may *smell* Seville oranges.

I see the column which we call our body as being an intricate computor—like a complex which no one—not even Freud, Jung or Ernest Jones—has been able to chart and to make a blueprint of.

When we talk of a writer's *perceptions*, we are up against this complex, this unexplored labyrinth (with no Ariadne to give us a ball of wool to find the way out): we are in it *alone*: for writing is *the* loneliest trade, and will permit no observer in its operation.

The writer who is *in-key* with his complex (though without being able to communicate what this in-keyness *is*) will suffer (and enjoy, and tolerate) certain Sympathies between his senses, certain Referred Pains: so that he may at last perceive the scent of blue, the touch of sound, and the taste of music.

The sympathies, or *pains*, of each sense will be referred to the other senses. But to the reader who is not a writer, is not in some degree alive to this complexity; the reader who judges everything by its rational content, its ability to make instant head-meaning; this reader will say that the writer has abused the truth, has not made sense.

Of course, I too believe that certain writers do not make sense: but I have been in the trade long enough to tell myself, at least, *why* they do not make sense. Broadly speaking, if they are honest craftsmen and creators, the two reasons are these:

(a) Words got the better of them—honest as the writers were.

(b) The writers used words because, like typewriting apes, they had learned how to put them down, but not how to *feel* them.

As a student, I was most impressed when a lecturer told

me that three chimpanzees, typing for a million years, would end up (by the law of averages, or permutations and combinations) with writing *Hamlet*. Or it may have been *King Lear*, I forget which. And I am not greatly bothered which. Psychological-statisticians can prove anything— like the Chancellor can prove that the cost of living has gone up by one per cent.

It is not the artist's function *to prove:* but *to create.* And, even if those poor apes *did* write Hamlet, they would not have created it. They would merely have (by some mathematical chance) *reproduced* it. If they had done that, as it were mechanically, one important factor would have been lacking: they would not have *felt* what they wrote, or have *perceived* what they wrote. To me, it is fundamental that the writer should have *feeling* about the thing he writes. He should suffer, experience and be aware of the forces that move him, and not be like one of those ancient Aeolian harps that hung on the antique mountains, vibrated by the breezes, and never hearing the music they themselves made.

I never thought to ask my lecturer about this when he first fed me the monkey-gimmick. But I would now: because it has long been an Article of Faith with me that the creative writer is born to awareness (if only partial) and to suffering (sometimes *in extremis*) just as the sparks fly upwards.

G

Bibliography

COMPILED BY ANTONY KAMM

A list of editions of works written or edited by Henry Treece and published in book form. A date in brackets denotes the date of a contract for an edition which had not yet been published at the time this monograph went to press. Many American editions of the novels contain variants from the texts originally published in the United Kingdom.

POETRY

38 Poems. Fortune Press, 1940
Towards a Personal Armageddon. James A. Decker, Illinois, U.S.A., 1941
Invitation and Warning. Faber, 1942
The Black Seasons. Faber, 1945
Collected Poems. Knopf, U.S.A., 1946
The Haunted Garden. Faber, 1947
The Exiles. Faber, 1952

CRITICISM

How I See Apocalypse. Drummond, 1946
Dylan Thomas : dog among the fairies. Drummond, 1949
  Benn *revised edition*, 1956
  De Graff, U.S.A., 1954; *revised edition*, 1956
  Shinko Shobo, Japan, 1967

PLAYS

Carnival King. Faber, 1955

NOVELS

I Cannot Go Hunting Tomorrow : short stories. Grey Walls Press, 1946
The Dark Island. Gollancz, 1952
  Bodley Head, 1958
  Random House, U.S.A., 1952
  As *The Savage Warriors*. Avon, U.S.A. *paperback*, 1959
The Rebels. Gollancz, 1953

The Golden Strangers. Bodley Head, 1956
  *Hodder and Stoughton *Library of Great Historical Novels*,
    1967 (with a foreword by Rosemary Sutcliff)
  Random House, U.S.A., 1957
  As *The Invaders.* Avon, U.S.A. p*aperback*, 1960
The Great Captains. Bodley Head, 1956
  Random House, U.S.A., 1956
  Fawcett (Crest), U.S.A. *paperback*, 1959
Red Queen, White Queen. Bodley Head, 1958
  Penguin *paperback*, 1962
  Random House, U.S.A., 1958
  As *The Pagan Queen.* Avon, U.S.A. *paperback*, 1959
A Fighting Man. Bodley Head, 1960
  As *The Master of Badger's Hall.* Random House, U.S.A., 1959
    Avon, U.S.A. *paperback*, 1961
Jason. Bodley Head, 1961
  New English Library *paperback*, 1963
  Sphere *paperback* (1969)
  Random House, U.S.A., 1961
  New American Library (Signet), U.S.A. *paperback*, 1962
  Paperback Library, U.S.A. *paperback*, 1969
Electra. Bodley Head, 1963
  Consul *paperback*, 1966
  Sphere *paperback*, 1968
  As *The Amber Princess.* Random House, U.S.A., 1962
    New American Library (Signet), U.S.A. *paperback*, 1964
Oedipus. Bodley Head, 1964
  Consul *paperback*, 1966
  Sphere *paperback*, 1968
  As *The Eagle King.* Random House, U.S.A., 1965
    New American Library (Signet), U.S.A. *paperback*, 1966
The Green Man. Bodley Head, 1966
  Sphere *paperback*, 1968
  Putnam, U.S.A., 1966

HISTORY

The Crusades. Bodley Head, 1962
  New English Library *paperback*, 1966

* Posthumously revised according to the author's wishes.

Random House, U.S.A., 1962
Mentor, U.S.A. *paperback*, 1964
As *De Kruistochten*. Hollandia, Holland, 1964
With Ewart Oakeshott *Fighting Men : how men have fought through the ages*. Brockhampton Press, 1963
Putnam, U.S.A., 1965

BOOKS EDITED BY HENRY TREECE
Herbert Read : an introduction. Faber, 1944
A Selection of Poems from Swinburne. Grey Walls Press, 1948

ANTHOLOGIES EDITED BY STEFAN SCHIMANSKI AND HENRY TREECE
Wartime Harvest. Bale and Staples, 1943
Transformation. Gollancz, 1943
A Map of Hearts : a collection of short stories. Drummond, 1944
Transformation Two. Drummond, 1944
Transformation Three. Drummond, 1945
Transformation Four. Drummond, 1947
Leaves in the Storm : a book of diaries. Drummond, 1947
New Romantic Anthology. Grey Walls Press, 1949

ANTHOLOGIES EDITED BY J. F. HENDRY AND HENRY TREECE
The New Apocalypse. Fortune Press, 1939
The White Horseman : prose and verse of the new apocalypse. Routledge, 1941

ANTHOLOGY EDITED BY JOHN PUDNEY AND HENRY TREECE
Air Force Poetry. Bodley Head, 1944

HISTORICAL NOVELS FOR CHILDREN
Legions of the Eagle Illustrated by Christine Price. Bodley Head, 1954
  Allen and Unwin *school edition*, 1954
  Transworld (Corgi) *paperback*, 1956
  Penguin (Puffin) *paperback*, 1965
The Eagles Have Flown Illustrated by Christine Price. Bodley Head, 1954
  Allen and Unwin *school edition*, 1954

Brockhampton Press (Knight) *paperback* (1966)

Viking's Dawn Illustrated by Christine Price. Bodley Head, 1955;
new format, 1969

Penguin (Puffin) *paperback*, 1967

Criterion, U.S.A., 1956

Schultz, Denmark (1968)

Hounds of the King Illustrated by Christine Price. Bodley Head,
1955

Longmans, Green *school edition*, 1965

Brockhampton Press (Knight) *paperback*, 1967

Schultz, Denmark (1968)

Men of the Hills Illustrated by Christine Price. Bodley Head, 1957

Criterion, U.S.A., 1958

As *Les Hommes des Collines*. Jeunesse, France, 1965

The Road to Miklagard Illustrated by Christine Price. Bodley
Head, 1957; *new format*, 1969

Penguin (Puffin) *paperback*, 1967

Criterion, U.S.A., 1957

Schultz, Denmark (1968)

The Children's Crusade Illustrated by Christine Price. Bodley
Head, 1958

Longmans, Green *school edition*, 1964

Penguin (Puffin) *paperback*, 1964

As *Perilous Pilgrimage*. Criterion, U.S.A., 1959

As *Der Kinder Kreuz Zug*. Räber, Switzerland, 1960

As *De Kinderkruishtoct*. De Kern, Holland, 1960

As *La Croisade des Enfants*. Alsatia, France, 1961

As *La Crusade de los Niños*. Mateu, Spain, 1963

Schultz, Denmark (1968)

The Return of Robinson Crusoe Illustrated by Will Nickless.
Hulton Press, 1958

As *Further Adventures of Robinson Crusoe*. Criterion, U.S.A.,
1958

The Bombard Illustrated by Christine Price. Bodley Head, 1959

As *Ride into Danger*. Criterion, U.S.A., 1959

Wickham and the Armada Illustrated by Hookway Cowles.
Hulton Press, 1959

Viking's Sunset Illustrated by Christine Price. Bodley Head, 1960;
new format, 1969

Penguin (Puffin) *paperback*, 1967
Criterion, U.S.A., 1960
Schultz, Denmark (1968)
Red Settlement. Bodley Head, 1960
The Golden One Illustrated by William Stobbs. Bodley Head, 1961
 Criterion, U.S.A., 1962
 As *Companheiros de Gengis Khan.* Brasiliense, Portugal, 1964
Man with a Sword Illustrated by William Stobbs. Bodley Head,
 1962
 Pantheon, U.S.A., 1964
War Dog Illustrated by Roger Payne. Brockhampton Press, 1962;
 new format, 1969
 Criterion, U.S.A., 1963
Horned Helmet Illustrated by Charles Keeping. Brockhampton
 Press, 1963
 University of London Press *school edition*, 1965
 Penguin (Puffin) *paperback*, 1965
 Criterion, U.S.A., 1963
 As *Horinghelm.* Malherbe, South Africa, 1963
 Dweumk, Yugoslavia (1966)
 Wolters, Holland (1967)
The Burning of Njal Illustrated by Bernard Blatch. Bodley Head,
 1964
 Criterion, U.S.A., 1964
The Last of the Vikings Illustrated by Charles Keeping. Brock-
 hampton Press, 1964
 Longmans, Green *school edition*, 1967
 As *The Last Viking.* Pantheon, U.S.A., 1966
 As *Die Laaste Wiking.* Malherbe, South Africa, 1966
 As *I Dorpens Tecken.* Natur och Kultur, Sweden, 1967
 Sauerlander, Germany (1968)
The Bronze Sword Illustrated by Mary Russon. Hamish Hamilton,
 1965
 As **The Centurion.* Duell, Sloane and Pearce, U.S.A., 1967
 As *Die Bronssward.* 'N Haum-Kinderbock, South Africa, 1969
Splintered Sword Illustrated by Charles Keeping. Brockhampton
 Press, 1965

* In a lengthened form.

Duell, Sloane and Pearce, U.S.A., 1966
   Avon (Camelot), U.S.A. *paperback*, 1967
The Queen's Brooch. Hamish Hamilton, 1966
   Penguin (Puffin) *paperback*, 1969
   Putnam, U.S.A., 1967
Swords from the North. Faber, 1967
   Pantheon, U.S.A., 1967
The Windswept City Illustrated by Faith Jaques. Hamish Hamilton, 1967
   Brockhampton Press (Knight) *paperback* (1967)
   Meredith, U.S.A., 1968
Vinland the Good Illustrated by William Stobbs. Map by Richard Treece. Bodley Head, 1967
   Penguin (Puffin) *paperback* (1968)
   As *Westward to Vinland.* S. G. Phillips, U.S.A., 1967
The Dream-Time Illustrated by Charles Keeping. Brockhampton Press 1967 (with a postscript by Rosemary Sutcliff)
   Meredith, U.S.A., 1968

THRILLERS FOR CHILDREN
Desperate Journey Illustrated by Richard Kennedy. Faber, 1954
Ask for King Billy Illustrated by Richard Kennedy. Faber, 1955; *paperback*, 1964
Hunter Hunted Illustrated by Richard Kennedy. Faber, 1957
   As *Jagttegn til Helvede.* Winther, Denmark, 1959
   As *Spion Bland Spioner.* Wennerberg, Sweden, 1959
Don't Expect Any Mercy. Faber, 1958
   As *L'Homme a la Jaguar Rouge.* Casterman, France, 1962
   As *Atom Spionen.* Winther, Denmark, 1959
   As *Vänta Ingen Nåd.* Wennerberg, Sweden, 1960
Killer in Dark Glasses. Faber, 1965
Bang You're Dead. Faber, 1966

MODERN FAMILY NOVEL FOR CHILDREN
The Jet Beads Illustrated by W. A. Sillince. Brockhampton Press, 1961

HISTORY FOR CHILDREN
Castles and Kings Illustrated by C. Walter Hodges. Batsford, 1959
   Criterion, U.S.A., 1960

The True Book about Castles Illustrated by G. H. Channing. Muller, 1960

Know about the Crusades. Blackie, 1963
  As *About the Crusades.* Dufour, Chester Springs, Pa., U.S.A., 1966

HISTORICAL STORIES AND ARTICLES COMMISSIONED FOR ANTHOLOGIES AND OTHER VOLUMES

Hereward the Wake. Glendower. In *Childcraft*, Field Enterprises, U.S.A. (1964)

Looking Around Castles. Children's Britannica *Extension Library*, 1964

Mithras, Lord of Light in *Miscellany Two*. Oxford University Press, 1965

The Black Longship in *Winter's Tales for Children 3*. Macmillan, 1967

C. S. Lewis

ROGER LANCELYN GREEN

To
JACK and JOY
in memory of
'A pub-crawl through the shining isles of Greece'

CONTENTS

1. Thulcandra

'Professor Lewis has read all the right books', wrote Marcus Crouch, 'but he is more than an imitator. He is a writer in the main stream of English fantasy, and he contributes to it his own clear and original spring.' While C. S. Lewis insisted that the waters of that spring—the books which he has added to our literary heritage—are all that concern us and all that we should judge him by, the modern trend in criticism (which he deplores in *The Personal Heresy* and other places) demands to know something about 'the right books'—whether in the form of actual literary influences, or influences of heredity, background and upbringing.

In the case of a writer of children's books there is certainly some excuse for curiosity about his own childhood, as about his own literary preferences and how he came to have them. 'I wrote the books I should have liked to read,' Lewis has admitted. 'That's always been my reason for writing. People won't write the books I want, so I have to do it for myself: no rot about "self-expression".'

Clive Staples Lewis was born on November 29, 1898, at Belfast, the son of a solicitor and of a clergyman's daughter— Flora Augusta Hamilton—who died when he was about nine. His father, Albert James Lewis, 'belonged to the first generation of his family that reached professional station', and was the son of a Welsh farmer who had emigrated to Ireland and risen to be a partner in a firm of 'Boiler-makers, Engineers, and Iron Ship Builders'. The Hamiltons had been clergymen, lawyers, sailors and the like for many generations, and 'through the Warrens the blood went back

to a Norman knight whose bones lie in Battle Abbey'—
the William de Warrenne of Kipling's 'Below the Mill
Dam'.

'The two families from which I spring were as different in
temperament as in origin,' wrote Lewis. 'My father's
people were true Welshmen, sentimental, passionate, and
rhetorical, easily moved both to anger and to tenderness;
men who laughed and cried a great deal and who had not
much of the talent for happiness. The Hamiltons were a
cooler race. Their minds were critical and ironic and they
had the talent for happiness in a high degree—went straight
for it as experienced travellers go for the best seat in a train.
From my earliest years I was aware of the vivid contrast
between my mother's cheerful and tranquil affection and
the ups and downs of my father's emotional life, and this
bred in me long before I was old enough to give it a name a
certain distrust or dislike of emotion as something uncomfortable and embarrassing and even dangerous.'

Until his mother's death Lewis lived a life of 'humdrum
and prosaic happiness' that 'awakes none of the poignant
nostalgia with which I look back on my much less happy
boyhood. It is not settled happiness but momentary joy
that glorifies the past.' Until he was seven Lewis lived in a
fairly small house, but then his father, prospering in the
world, built a much larger home: 'The New House is
almost a major character in my story,' wrote Lewis. 'I am a
product of long corridors, empty sunlit rooms, upstair
indoor silences, attics explored in solitude, distant noises of
gurgling cisterns and pipes, and the noise of wind under the
tiles. Also, of endless books. My father bought all the books
he read and never got rid of any of them. There were books
in the study, books in the drawing-room, books in the
cloakroom, books (two deep) in the great bookcase on the

landing, books in a bedroom, books piled as high as my shoulder in the cistern attic, books of all kinds reflecting every transient stage of my parents' interests, books readable and unreadable, books suitable for a child and books most emphatically not. Nothing was forbidden me. In the seemingly endless rainy afternoons I took volume after volume from the shelves. I had always the same certainty of finding a book that was new to me as a man who walks into a field has of finding a new blade of grass.'

The more literary of the adult books were the works of the novelists and humorists, there was very little poetry. Neither his father nor his mother 'had the least taste for that kind of literature to which my allegiance was given the moment I could choose books for myself. Neither had ever listened to the horns of elfland. There was no copy of either Keats or Shelley in the house, and the copy of Coleridge was never (to my knowledge) opened. If I am a romantic my parents bear no responsibility for it.'

More important for the future creator of Narnia were the few children's books which played an important part in opening early windows into 'faerie lands forlorn'. His first glimpses of the world of chivalry came by way of Conan Doyle's *Sir Nigel* and Mark Twain's perverted Arthuriad *A Yankee at the Court of King Arthur*. But 'much better than either of these was E. Nesbit's trilogy, *Five Children and It*, *The Phoenix and the Carpet*, and *The Amulet*. The last did most for me. It first opened my eyes to antiquity, the "dark backward and abysm of time". I can still re-read it with delight. *Gulliver* in an unexpurgated and lavishly illustrated edition was one of my favourites, and I pored endlessly over an almost complete set of old *Punches* which stood in my father's study. Tenniel gratified my passion for "dressed animals" with his Russian Bear, British Lion, Egyptian

Crocodile and the rest . . . Then came the Beatrix Potter books, and here at last beauty.'

A peculiarly unpleasant picture of a stag-beetle with movable horns threatening a midget child on a toadstool, gave Lewis his earliest nightmares, and a lifelong antipathy to insects—'Their angular limbs, their jerky movements, their dry, metallic noises, all suggest either machines that have come to life or life degenerating into mechanism.' But Lewis was always fond of animals, even though at first he knew them mainly through the medium of books and pre-ferred them anthropomorphised and even dressed as humans.

Animals of this kind were the theme of his earliest stories which were themselves preceded by drawings, and he very soon invented 'Animal-Land' to be his imaginary kingdom—no connection, apparently, with Sybil Corbet's *Animal-Land Where there are No People* (1897), also invented by a child. 'Most of us have a secret country,' he confesses in *The Voyage of the 'Dawn Treader'*.

The incentives to have a country, to draw it and to write about it seem to have come from his brother, Warren, three years his senior but from the first his closest friend and more so after their mother's death in the long hours during which they were left to their own devices while their father was at work. His brother's country was India, in which he specialised with all the intenseness of a child's enthusiasm so well described in *Dream Days*, but which formed also a part of the imaginary world in which Animal-Land was situated. And it led to a far less literary and more historical inspiration, the very choice of locale revealing the boy who afterwards became a regular army officer and finally an out-standing historian of the France of Louis XIV.

The younger boy's enthusiasms were literary and roman-

tic from the first. 'What drove me to write was the extreme
manual clumsiness from which I have always suffered . . .
With pencil and pen I was handy enough, and I can still tie
as good a bow as ever lay on a man's collar; but with a tool
or a bat or a gun, a sleeve-link or a corkscrew, I have always
been unteachable. It was this that forced me to write. I
longed to make things, ships, houses, engines . . . I was
driven to write stories instead; little dreaming to what a
world of happiness I was being admitted. You can do more
with a castle in a story than with the best cardboard castle
that ever stood on a nursery table.' The first stories 'were an
attempt to combine my two chief literary pleasures—
"dressed animals" and "knights-in-armour". As a result, I
wrote about chivalrous mice and rabbits who rode out in
complete mail to kill not giants but cats. But already the
mood of the systemiser was strong in me; the mood which
led Trollope so endlessly to elaborate his Barsetshire. The
Animal-Land which came into action in the holidays when
my brother was at home was a modern Animal-Land; it had
to have trains and steamships if it was to be a country
shared with him. It followed, of course, that the medieval
Animal-Land about which I wrote my stories must be the
same country in an earlier period; and of course the two
periods must be properly connected. This led me from
romancing to historiography; I set about writing a full
history of Animal-Land . . .' So a whole world grew, and
for many years 'those parts of that world which we regarded
as our own—Animal-Land and India—were increasingly
populated with consistent characters'.

The death of their mother and a certain lack of understanding which grew between them and their father, drove
the Lewis boys deeper into their imaginative world, and
caused the younger to spend more and more time alone,

seeking 'the sure companionship of books' rather than the society of his contemporaries.

School came when Lewis was just under ten. Hitherto he had been taught by his mother and an excellent governess. The school, at which his brother was already a pupil, was in England, and was run by a sadist drifting gradually into insanity: the rigours and eccentricities of Rodwell Regis as described by Anstey in *Vice Versa*—'the only truthful school story in existence,' Lewis calls it—were mild and commonplace to the terrors of this Belsen with its continuous floggings and its lack of amenities both civilised and educational. 'At that school as I knew it most boys learned nothing and no boy learned much.' It seems remarkable that Mr Lewis senior did not discover the state of affairs: but boys are muter than oysters under such conditions. The parallel with Kipling in the 'House of Desolation' at Southsea is interesting.

In 1910 the school closed, and after a short spell as a weekly boarder at Campbell College in Belfast, Lewis was sent to another prep school, at Malvern this time, his brother being already at the great public school near by.

It was at this time that Lewis was first inspired and enslaved by the magic of the North: 'pure "Northerness" engulfed me: a vision of huge, clear spaces hanging above the Atlantic in the endless twilight of Northern summer, remoteness, severity'. He came to this passion by way of retellings of the *Ring* cycle with Rackham's illustrations, and by records of Wagner's music, leading to the entranced study of the Prose and Verse *Eddas* and of such Sagas as had been translated, and of all things 'Northern', including, a little later, the prose romances of William Morris and his *Sigurd the Volsung*. And now his own writings turned from the histories of Animal-Land to the compilation of great epics of Norse mythology. Had not chance turned some of his enthusiasm in the direction of the Greek and Latin Classics, the 'Northerness' might have formed the background of his later imaginative writings, as in the parallel case of E. R. Eddison who was caught by the same magic after reading Haggard's *Eric Brighteyes*, but then taught himself Old Norse and went to Iceland. Eddison's *The Worm Ouroboros* (1922) became later one of Lewis's favourite books; but in his own imaginative work the strongest sensation of an underlying 'Northerness' comes, most unexpectedly, in his story based on a Greek legend, *Till We Have Faces* (1956). There are, however, provocative echoes of the North throughout the Narnian stories.

When Lewis proceeded to Malvern College in the autumn of 1913, it was with a Classical entrance scholarship to his credit; and though he detested his experiences of a public school almost more than even those of his earlier prep school, his brightest memory was of the classics master, who 'taught us Latin and Greek, but everything else came in incidentally'. Perhaps also the courtesy which is so marked a characteristic of Lewis's critical writings stems, or was at least brought out by this master: 'His manner was perfect: no familiarity, no hostility, no threadbare humour; mutual respect, decorum. "Never let us live with *amousia*", was one of his favourite maxims: *amousia*, the absence of the Muses. And he knew, as Spenser knew, that courtesy was of the Muses.'

From his year at Malvern dates Lewis's knowledge and detestation of the 'Inner Ring' approach to life which he was to expose so devastatingly in *That Hideous Strength* (1945), so much of which turns on Mark Suddock's miserable attempts to get into the Inner Rings at Bracton and Belbury. He looked back on it as a purgatory of false values, noise and increasing weariness, but with the private world of the imagination assuming almost a morbid importance—the 'moments when you were too happy to speak, when the gods and heroes rioted through your head, when satyrs danced and Maenads roamed on the mountains, when Brynhild and Sieglinde, Deirdre, Maeve and Helen were all about you, till sometimes you felt that it might break you with mere richness'.

At home the period was signalised by the first close friendship, with a boy a few years older who had the same interests in Norse mythology and romantic literature. This was all the more welcome as Lewis was experiencing a temporary loss of the close relations with his brother, now a Sandhurst cadet, who had thoroughly enjoyed Malvern.

In the autumn of 1914 Lewis having persuaded his father to take him away from Malvern, began on the most formative part of his education, as a private pupil with a retired schoolmaster at Great Bookham in Surrey: W. T. Kirkpatrick, 'a rigid logician', who supplied the basis for the character of MacPhee in *That Hideous Strength*. 'If ever a man came near to being a purely logical entity, that man was Kirk', wrote Lewis. 'The idea that human beings should exercise their vocal organs for any purpose except that of communicating or discovering truth was to him preposterous. The most casual remark was taken as a summons to disputation.' This keen, analytical habit of thought Lewis made his own, and it is particularly conspicuous in his writings on religion (notably in the broadcast talks collected as *Mere Christianity*), and in his critical and scholarly books and lectures. Its application made him also one of the best and most stimulating tutors at Oxford during his thirty years at Magdalen College.

On the literary and academic side Kirkpatrick had almost as profound an effect. His method of teaching suited Lewis exactly. With no more than the average schoolboy grounding in Greek on his side, they began with Homer, and went straight into the *Iliad* without preparation, Kirkpatrick reading the Greek out loud to begin with. 'He then translated with a few, a very few, explanations, about a hundred lines. I had never seen a classical author taken in such large gulps before. When he had finished he handed me over Crusius' *Lexicon* and, having told me to go through again as much as I could of what he had done, left the room. It seemed an odd method of teaching, but it worked. At first I could travel only a very short way along the trail he had blazed, but every day I could travel farther. Presently I could travel the whole way . . . He appeared at this stage to value speed more than absolute accuracy. The great gain was that I very soon became able to understand a great deal without (even mentally) translating it; I was beginning to think in Greek. That is the great Rubicon to cross in learning any language.'

French literature was treated in the same way, and 'later in my career we branched out into German and Italian. Here his methods were the same. After the very briefest contact with Grammars and exercises I was plunged into *Faust* and the *Inferno* . . . But Homer came first. Day after day and month after month we drove gloriously onward, tearing the whole *Achilleid* out of the *Iliad* and tossing the rest on one side, and then reading the *Odyssey* entire, till the music of the thing and the clear, bitter brightness that lives in almost every formula had become part of me.'

The long procession of peaceful, well-regulated days also had a lasting effect on Lewis. Work all morning; a solitary walk all afternoon; work between tea and dinner, and then talk and discussion until bedtime became his ideally apportioned day.

Solitary walks in the vividly contrasting settings of term-time Surrey and holiday Ulster brought a strong apprecia-tion of nature and of natural beauties: the visible scenery depicted in a few perfectly chosen words in the Narnian stories, and the precise, unstudied descriptions of animal life. 'I measured distances by the standard of man, man walking on his two feet, not by the standard of the internal combustion engine. I had not been allowed to deflower the very idea of distance; in return I possessed "infinite riches" in what would have been to motorists "a little room". The truest and most horrible claim made for modern transport is that it "annihilates space". It does. It annihilates one of the most glorious gifts we have been given. It is a vile inflation which lowers the value of distance, so that a modern boy travels a hundred miles with less sense of liberation and pilgrimage and adventure than his grandfather got from travelling ten.'

So Lewis's troubled boyhood ended in the peace and purpose of the three years in Surrey, and having taken a scholarship in Classics, he went up to University College, Oxford, in the summer of 1917. He entered, however, into anything but peace, knowing that he would soon be wafted away into the horrors of the Great War. He reached the front line trenches on his nineteenth birthday as a second-lieutenant in the Somerset Light Infantry, and was wounded in front of Lillers in April 1918. He was demobilised after passing through a convalescent camp, and returned to Oxford in January 1919—of which he wrote in his first published book, a little volume of poems that appeared later the same year:

We are not wholely brute. To us remains
A clean, sweet city lulled by ancient streams,
A place of vision and of loosening chains,
A refuge of the elect, a tower of dreams.

11. Perelandra

The brief sketch of C. S. Lewis's life before reaching Oxford early in his twenty-first year has of necessity omitted much of importance—which may be read in his autobiographic volume *Surprised by Joy: The Shape of My Early Life* (1955). The most important omissions are of how he lapsed from the Christianity in which he had been brought up, into Agnosticism and then straight Atheism, and of the recurrent experience of Joy which gives its name to the title. His spiritual pilgrimage down into Atheism and back 'from Popular Realism to Philosophical Idealism; from Idealism to Pantheism; from Pantheism to Theism; and from Theism to Christianity' must be sought in his own books: directly in *Surprised by Joy*, obliquely in *Mere Christianity* and his other religious books, and more or less allegorically in his early narrative poem *Dymer* (1926), still definitely anti-religious, to the triumphant conclusion in his prose 'Allegorical Apology for Christianity, Reason and Romanticism', *The Pilgrim's Regress* (1933).

It would be hard to say what effect his experiences of Joy have had on his writings, and rash, indeed impossible, to point to places in his works which have brought or could bring a similar experience to a reader. Even to describe the experience is difficult and dangerous. The apparent cause may be a natural scene, a line of poetry, a name: the sensation is as of a moment of intense longing, a pain and a pleasure in one, almost too strong to bear—lost the moment it is found, and irrecoverable by any conscious means: the longing may be longed for in the ordinary way, but it cannot be induced. It has something of Wordsworth's 'Intimations of Immortality', of Andrew Lang's 'A pang, a sacred memory of prayer'; it has been described as a reflection from the unseen world caught for a moment in an earthly mirror. Lewis, drawing from personal experience (and it must be emphasised that none of the causes will work again, and few of them will work on anyone else) speaks of it as 'that unnameable something, desire for which pierces us like a rapier at the smell of a bonfire, the sound of wild ducks flying overhead, the title of *The Well at the World's End*, the opening lines of *Kubla Khan*, the morning cobwebs in late summer, or the noise of falling waves'. Perhaps another experience of it is behind H. G. Wells's *Door in the Wall*, even behind Lob's Wood in *Dear Brutus*— for neither are there when they are sought for, and are indeed only present in 'heaven-sent moments', and only for those for whom they are intended. More reference to Joy would be to go beyond the scope of the present monograph, but it could not be omitted altogether by one who experienced one of these moments from Outside when first reading *Out of the Silent Planet* in 1938.

On the more mundane level, Lewis took a First Class degree in Classical Moderations in 1920, and a First in 'Greats' in 1922. Then, so as to have a second string to his bow, he read the English School, and took a First in that also, in 1923. The following year he acted as a substitute for E. F. Carritt, the Philosophy Tutor at University College, and in 1925 was elected Fellow and Tutor in English Literature at Magdalen, a position which he held until he was made Professor of Medieval and Renaissance Literature at Cambridge in 1954. At Cambridge he became a Fellow of Magdalene, and on relinquishing his Fellowship at Magdalen, Oxford, was made an Honorary Fellow of his old college. Of the many other honours and degrees which later came his way, that of Hon. Doctor of Divinity at St Andrews is the most unusual, as Lewis is almost the only man not in Holy Orders to receive it. (Andrew Lang was also made a D.D., but in his case it was conferred by Breslau University, where apparently the custom was not so unusual.)

In 1957 Lewis married the American poetess Joy David-man who was dying of cancer of the bone. Though not expected to live a year, she made an amazing recovery—'the nearest thing to a miracle I have ever experienced,' Lewis called it—and gave him over two years of supremely happy married life. Early in 1960 the disease broke out again; she was well enough for a trip to Greece, Rhodes and Crete in April (Lewis's only experience of foreign travel) but died two months later.

Lewis's own health broke down shortly after this, and after an almost fatal illness in June 1963 he resigned his Chair at Cambridge and retired to his home at Headington Quarry, Oxford. On November 22 of the same year he died suddenly and painlessly.

As a teacher, Lewis proved to be one of the most success-ful and stimulating tutors of his time, and his lectures were for some years the most popular in Oxford, certainly in the English School. His closest rivals in popularity during at least the middle period of his tutorship were Lascelles Abercrombie and Charles Williams; and though at their best moments they may have woken deeper responses in the minds of their hearers, Lewis surpassed them both as a sheer transmitter of knowledge in a form so interesting that many students attended the same course of lectures more than once for the fascination of what he told, and the ad-mirable and amusing way in which it was 'put across'. The

usual courses were prolegomena to Medieval and to Renaissance studies (the basis of his last book, *The Discarded
Image*, 1964); the series that afterwards became *A Preface to
Paradise Lost* (1942); and miscellaneous lectures (some
subsequently published) on such subjects as *Hamlet*, or the
poems of Charles Williams.

Apart from the two early volumes of verse, and the prose
allegory *Pilgrim's Regress*, Lewis's first book was *The Allegory
of Love* (1936), which won him the Hawthornden Prize.
This is one of the outstanding works of literary scholarship, a study of the Medieval tradition of 'Courtly Love'
from Ovid to Spenser. The *Preface to Paradise Lost* is
almost as notable—a work which Gordon Bottomley said
ought to be on the desks of all would-be poets, in company
with Bridges' *Milton's Prosody*. His most sustained work of
scholarship is the volume in the Oxford History of English
Literature, in seven hundred pages, covering *The Sixteenth
Century, Excluding Drama*, which was published in 1954;
and almost his last and most provocative was the little
Experiment in Criticism of 1961.

Though the Narnian stories may be beginning to usurp
its place, as their first readers grow up, C. S. Lewis is
generally best known as a writer for *The Screwtape Letters*
(1942), the wise and witty correspondence of an elderly
devil, Screwtape, with his young nephew Wormwood on
the best means of tempting the Human who has been
allotted to him and bringing him to 'Our Father Below'. Its
object was, of course, the reverse of its form: 'its purpose
was not to speculate about diabolical life but to throw light
from a new angle on the life of men'. Screwtape's instructions to Wormwood, and his comments on Wormwood's
failures or successes, bring out in a vivid and unexpected
way Man's daily temptations, and show in which hidden,

insidious and apparently innocent forms they can come.

The Screwtape Letters was a best-seller, and raised Lewis to the position of one of our best-known living authors—at once among the most praised and the most criticised. He had already written one book on a theological subject, *The Problem of Pain* (1940), and as his 'war-work' he toured R.A.F. camps giving simple lectures on theology, followed by questions and discussions. At this time also he gave the short weekly talks over the B.B.C. which were collected as *Broadcast Talks* (1942), *Christian Behaviour* (1943) and *Beyond Personality* (1944) and later revised in one volume as *Mere Christianity* (1952). In these the deceptive simplicity and obviousness hide a depth of understanding which by reminding the Believer and making the Unbeliever think, have had a wide and beneficial effect, and deservedly earned their author the name of 'Apostle to the Sceptics'. *Miracles* (1947), his next theological work, was much more difficult for the ordinary reader, but later books such as *Reflections on the Psalms* (1958), *The Four Loves* (1960) and *Letters to Malcolm: Chiefly on Prayer* (published early in 1964, a few months after his death), are models of simple persuasiveness and clear reasoning. *The Great Divorce* (1945), religious instruction cast in the form of a story, returned more to the *genre* of *Screwtape*, and was even preferred to it by some readers (its author included).

Also during the war Lewis consented to preach occasionally, usually at Oxford; he and the late Archbishop Temple were said to be the only two who could fill the University Church to capacity. Most impressive of all was his sermon preached one Whit Sunday at Mansfield College Chapel which one who heard it described as 'like hearing St Paul'.

Most of Lewis's books so far mentioned are definitely intended for older readers, though *The Screwtape Letters* might appeal to those in their teens, and *Mere Christianity* should be read and re-read by all young people before Confirmation.

But the Apostle to the Sceptics and the Romancer (if his shade will forgive a term which he rightly condemned as too general), whom we have already seen joining hands in *Screwtape* and *The Great Divorce*, met and became one in the trilogy of 'mythic fantasies' which began quite quietly with *Out of the Silent Planet* in 1938.

'What immediately spurred me to write', Lewis told a then unknown correspondent at the time, 'was Olaf Stapledon's *Last and First Men* and an essay in J. B. S. Haldane's *Possible Worlds*, both of which seemed to take the idea of such [Space] travel seriously and to have the desperately immoral outlook which I try to pillory in Weston. I like the whole interplanetary idea as a *mythology* and simply wished to conquer for my own (Christian) point of view what has always hitherto been used by the opposite side. I think Wells's *First Men in the Moon* the best of the sort I have read . . .'

And on the general subject of romances of other worlds he wrote in his essay 'On Stories' (1947):

'No merely physical strangeness or merely spatial distance will realise that idea of otherness which is what we are always trying to grasp in a story about voyaging through Space: you must go into another dimension. To construct plausible and moving "other worlds" you must draw on the only real "other world" we know, that of the spirit.'

From these basic ideas Lewis built first *Out of the Silent Planet*, and then, going farther into the other world of the spirit, its sequel *Perelandra* (1943). The first begins like an ordinary space-thriller. Dr Ransom, a Cambridge philologist, is kidnapped by the two scientists Weston and Devine, who have already built their space-ship and visited Mars in it. They take him to the Red Planet, convinced that the inhabitants require an earth-man as a sacrifice. On Mars, Ransom escapes from his captors, but like them flees in terror from any possible Martians:

'His mind, like so many minds of his generation, was richly furnished with bogies. He had read his H. G. Wells and others. His universe was peopled with horrors such as ancient and medieval mythology could hardly rival. No insect-like, vermiculate or crustacean Abominable, no monstrous union of superhuman intelligence and insatiable cruelty seemed to him anything but likely on an alien world.'

The memorable and enthralling thing about Ransom's adventures on Malacandra is his slow discovery of the true nature of the three forms of Intelligent Beings who dwell there. Of these, the first and the most fully established in our understandings are the country-dwelling and naturally poetic *hrossa*; the *pfifltriggi* are the artificers, and the *sorns* are the intellectuals. The climax is reached when he is brought before the Oyarsa of Malacandra, who is the 'Intelligence' of the planet, and learns that Mars has not fallen, but is still in the state of innocence in which Earth would have been had the Fall of Man not occurred. For the Earth, Thulcandra, is the 'Silent Planet' of the title, and is cut off from the spiritual life and control still flourishing in the rest of the Field of Arbol, the Solar System, each planet ruled by its Eldil (Angel or Intelligence or Viceroy of God): the viceroy of Earth is the Bent Eldil, the fallen angel who rebelled against God. And while the Oyarsa of Malacandra has much to tell Ransom of unfallen creation, he has to learn from him of the supreme act of the Incarnation which has taken place only in the Silent Planet.

Out of the Silent Planet appeals strongly to the boy reader, just as Wells's *First Men in the Moon* does: more strongly to those to whom imagination means more than science, but to both for the thrilling story and to such of its special excellences as suit their mental or spiritual palates. '*Out of the Silent Planet*', wrote Marjorie Hope Nicholson, after studying all the earlier literature of what we now call Science Fiction, 'is to me the most beautiful of all cosmic voyages and in some ways the most moving.'

A little more difficult for the young reader, but an incomparably more important book is *Perelandra*, which takes us one step farther. Ransom and the two scientists had returned to Earth at the end of the previous book: but now that Ransom has once passed out of the shadow of the Silent Planet, the spiritual messengers can visit him even when he has returned. For this reason, indeed, his visit to Mars was permitted. Now they take him (by frankly supernatural means) to Venus, whose real name in the Field of Arbol is Perelandra—at once the planet and its Intelligence, of whom Aphrodite and Venus are but dim reflections seen in the distorting mirrors of the Bent Hnau—fallen mankind —of Thulcandra.

Arrived on Perelandra, Ransom finds it at the exact stage which Earth had reached when Adam and Eve lived in the Garden of Eden and Satan had not yet entered into the serpent. The imagination, the conception, the description of the Perelandran Paradise in which Ransom finds himself is astonishing and awe-inspiring: Lewis has depicted Venus once and for all, and it is impossible not to believe his picture —or to get it out of our minds and visual memories once it has been imprinted there. It is impossible to capture it in a short quotation: the golden sky, the floating islands that undulate with the waves, the differences of a Perelandran thunder-storm, the flowers, the fauna—the whole realisation of another world.

In this Paradise Ransom meets Perelandra's equivalent of Eve, the Green Lady (separated for the moment, as Eve was, from her Adam, 'the King'), and soon realises why he has been sent to this 'the first of worlds to wake after the great change' of the Incarnation. For suddenly Weston appears in his space-ship, which, Ransom feels, is dangerous enough. But before long the terrible truth dawns on him and us: Weston in his space-ship is but the vehicle, the Trojan Horse, by means of which the Devil, the Bent Eldil, has penetrated the defences of Perelandra as he once made his way into Eden in the form of a serpent.

The main portion of the book is taken up with 'Weston's' siege of the lady and Ransom's attempts to foil him, by reason at first, and at last by force in an epic battle that has echoes of *Beowulf*. And finally comes the great scene of triumph when the safety of Perelandra has been assured for all time:

'The apotheosis at the end of the book is one of the finest efforts of recent fiction', wrote R. B. McCallum. 'In a vale of the Great Mountain, surrounded by light other than that of Arbol the Sun, the King and the Lady, triumphant over evil, take delivery of their world from the eldils of Malacandra and Perelandra, now for once assuming human form, gigantic, resplendent and beautiful with a terrible purity, Ares and Aphrodite such as no poet or artist has ever been able to conceive, while Ransom hears their message and sustains the experience not so much by knowledge and virtue as by that simplicity of heart which Grace can confer upon a Christian man. Not all readers will have their imaginations configured to the medium of Mr Lewis's expression, whether through too little or too great a share of the imaginative faculty. Those who are susceptible to this style and can bring themselves to consider this doctrine will find in *Perelandra* a very considerable experience.'

The third book of the trilogy, *That Hideous Strength* (1945), need not be considered here at much length, since it is entirely adult. It is, as its sub-title tells us, 'A modern fairy-tale for grown-ups', taking place on this earth and in the modern world, but showing how an attempt by the powers of evil was foiled by Ransom and a few of the chosen who were drawn to him for this special purpose. It is a long book, but the interest is caught on the first page, and grows throughout with no slackening, so that it is hard to put it down even at a third or fourth reading: at a first it is quite impossible. In taking a perfectly ordinary not very happily married couple, attached to a small university near which the vast and soulless National Institute of Co-ordinated Experiments is about to be built, and then introducing the elements of wonder and the spiritual powers by a gradual infiltration, *That Hideous Strength* recalls the methods of Charles Williams in his 'spiritual thrillers', and indeed it has been described as 'a Charles Williams novel written by C. S. Lewis'. The likeness is only of tone and method, but the influence may be there, since at the time of writing Williams had become one of Lewis's closest friends, and for several years they and J. R. R. Tolkien would meet weekly to read and discuss what each was writing—Lewis *Perelandra* and *That Hideous Strength*, Williams *All Hallow's Eve*, and Tolkien the earlier parts of *The Lord of the Rings*.

Lewis's only other adult story, *Till We Have Faces* (1956), a strange, compelling and quite unexpected version of the Cupid and Psyche legend, cannot be considered here either. Lewis describes it as a 'straight tale of barbarism, the mind of an ugly woman, dark idolatry and pale enlightenment at war with each other and with vision, and the havoc which a vocation, or even a faith, works on human life'. For the older reader it is one of his most interesting books, and the most thought-provoking. It lacks the enchantment of Malacandra and Perelandra; it catches the intellect powerfully, but hardly touches the heart—but nevertheless in it, even if less strongly than in others, we feel, like Ransom, 'a sensation not of following an adventure but of enacting a myth'.

III. Narnia

'Were all the things which appeared as mythology on Earth scattered through other worlds as realities?' Ransom asks himself in *Perelandra*; and as we read the seven volumes of the Chronicles of Narnia we are inclined to feel that they were inspired or suggested by some such question.

Lewis is not only a myth-maker but a myth-user, and this stands him in good stead in Narnia which is very much the land where the myths are still living. On Perelandra Ransom felt that he had found the dragon-guarded Tree of the Hesperides—and remembered that he had seen the Cyclops on Malacandra, a one-eyed giant living in a cave and tending his flocks. The deeper use of myth ties in with Lewis's belief as to the relation between the great pagan mythologies and Christianity: 'Where has religion reached its true maturity? Where have the hints of all Paganism been fulfilled?' Or as an Atheist once remarked to him: 'Rum thing, all that about the Dying God. Seems to have really happened once.'

We get near to the feeling in a scrap of dialogue from *That Hideous Strength*, just before the awakening of Merlin:

' "There used to be things on this earth pursuing their own business, so to speak. They weren't ministering spirits sent to help fallen humanity, but neither were they enemies preying upon us. Even in St Paul one gets glimpses of a population that won't exactly fit into our two columns of angels and devils. And if you go back farther—all the gods, elves, dwarfs, water-people, *fatæ*, *longævi*. You and I know too much to think they are just illusions."

"You think there are things like that?"

"I think there were. I think there was room for them then, but the universe has come more to a point. Not all rational things perhaps. Some would be mere wills inherent in matter, hardly conscious. More like animals. Others— but I don't really know. At any rate, that is the sort of situation in which one got a man like Merlin." '

This background of thought is apparent throughout the Narnian stories, and for this reason it is of little importance to look for 'sources' and 'originals'. Such research might tell us what books Lewis had read, and where some of his ideas came from: but pure invention is almost impossible, and all authors receive their inspiration with the aid of suggestions or trains of thought induced by the odd word, line, sentence or even idea in another man's book—or in the general background of myth from which as often as not the previous writer himself had drawn.

What matters is the use made of these hints, ideas and inspirations—these pieces of coloured glass in the kaleidoscope, which are the old, universal pieces, but now arranged in a new pattern.

Lewis's use of myth in making his new mythology covers all such 'borrowings' and turns them to glorious account. We cannot accuse him of unoriginality when he introduces fauns, satyrs, centaurs, giants, Father Christmas, and the rest: he meant to introduce them, he wants us to recognise old friends, their introduction is part of the whole 'build-up', and the literary echoes are just as much a part of it: our pleasure is increased if we recognise or half-recognise them, it is all part of the magic which makes Narnia so intensely real and so much a re-discovery rather than a discovery.

Thus one can point out how closely the description of the

Sea Serpent in *The Voyage of the 'Dawn Treader'* echoes that by Kipling of the same creature in 'A Matter of Fact', or find a passage in Lucian's *Vera Historia* which may have suggested the Monopods, or underline a paragraph in *Prince Caspian* which is based on *The Princess and Curdie*, or wonder whether the moving trees were inspired by an early reading of *The Lord of the Rings* in manuscript—or Arthur Rackham's illustrations to *Peter Pan in Kensington Gardens*.

'Whenever he sets to work to create', wrote Haggard of Andrew Lang, 'his wide knowledge and his marvellous memory of everything he has read—and little worth studying in ancient or modern literature has escaped him—prove positive stumbling-blocks in his path'. It is a sign of Lewis's greatness as a creator in this sense that he can make the same 'stumbling-blocks' the very corner stones of his edifice: and he was a builder who rejected no good stones.

More interesting are the unconscious parallels, though their application is of general rather than particular importance. Thus the boatload of pirates got into Narnia, as described in *Prince Caspian*, in precisely the same way as the crew of corsairs got into the Land at the Earth's Core in Edgar Rice Burroughs' *Tanar of Pellucidar* (1930): but it is quite certain that Lewis had never heard of this obscure and inferior work of fiction which has not even been published in this country.

Of more interest is the entrance into Narnia through the Wardrobe in the Spare Room—'the far land of Spare Oom . . . the bright city of War Drobe', as Mr Tumnus the Faun calls them. For it was by the same door that Amabel went into her magic world ('the station was *Bigwardrobeinspare-room*') in E. Nesbit's story *The Aunt and Amabel*, which, though he agreed that he must have read it, Lewis had certainly forgotten when he sent the Pevensies into Narnia by the same door. (The story was collected in *The Magic World* (1912), too late to have been a childhood book for him; but he may have come across it at its first appearance in *Blackie's Children's Annual* (1909), published in time for Christmas 1908 when he was just ten.)

Whether or not he had read this particular story, the influence of E. Nesbit is obvious and admitted. In his book on Lewis as a theological writer, published (in America only) in 1949, Chad Walsh says, when dealing with possible books to come, 'He talks vaguely of completing a children's book which he has begun "in the tradition of E. Nesbit".'

This referred to the first few chapters of *The Lion, the Witch and the Wardrobe*, a story which had been forming in his mind for some time, but of which only a little had been written down, but then set aside owing to criticism from one of his older friends by then rather out of touch with children and their books, and wedded to different modes of thought where fairy-tale and fantasy were concerned. However, the story was not to be kept down; by March 1949 he was working on it again, and reading the early chapters to another friend, who proved more encouraging—and perhaps saw more clearly that here was the beginning of a really new and exciting development in children's literature. The sequel, *Prince Caspian*, was written by the end of the year, and 1950 must have been spent by Lewis largely in exploring and living in the new world which had, as it were, been shown to him: for by the time *The Lion, the Witch and the Wardrobe* was published that autumn, *The Voyage of the 'Dawn Treader'* and *The Horse and his Boy* were finished, and *The Silver Chair* nearing completion. After this there was a pause, much longer being spent on *The Magician's Nephew*, which was not completed until the end of 1951, to be followed by the final instalment, *The Last Battle*, written two years later.

'In a certain sense, I have never actually "made" a story,' wrote Lewis, when looking back on the seven Chronicles of Narnia. 'With me the process is much more like bird-watching than either talking or building. I see pictures. Some of these pictures have a common flavour, almost a common smell, which groups them together. Keep quiet and watch and they will begin joining themselves up. If you were very lucky (I have never been as lucky as all that) a whole set might join themselves so consistently that there you had a complete story: without doing anything yourself. But more often (in my experience always) there are gaps. Then at last you have to do some deliberate inventing, have to contrive reasons why these characters should be in these various places doing these various things. I have no idea whether this is the usual way of writing stories, still less whether it is the best. It is the only one I know: images always come first.'

The proper reason, moreover, for writing children's stories is he insists, 'because a children's story is the best art-form for something you have to say: just as a composer might write a Dead March not because there was a public funeral in view but because certain musical ideas that had occurred to him went best into that form'.

To describe the Chronicles of Narnia is to give little idea of their quality. At the most obvious level they are a series of adventure stories told by a master story-teller with an excellent sense of construction. Except for *The Voyage of the 'Dawn Treader'*, which is a series of adventures as Caspian and his companions voyage from island to island on their quest, each book is a carefully unfolding whole, built up with an instinctive touch from a prosaic beginning and so guided gently and persuasively into the heart of the marvels that coincides with the climax of the adventure. Looking a little deeper, we find that the magic is not only that of the wonders themselves: there is a 'glamour' in the old sense that falls upon us as we enter Narnia, like the softest dew, but growing as we venture deeper and deeper in. This is the subtle creation of atmosphere, of which the sights, the sounds, the smell and taste and feel grow upon us until Narnia becomes a place that we remember or recognise rather than learn about.

Deeper still, and we realise a difference between these stories and most other children's books: though the White Witch or Miraz may represent the evil power, just as there are good powers culminating in Aslan, the real villains as well as the real heroes and heroines are among the children who find their way or are drawn into Narnia. It is Edmund who betrays Peter, Susan and Lucy to the Witch, just as it is Eustace who is the disruptive element on board the *Dawn Treader*. But, to get even nearer to the heart of the matter, although they bring about the peripeties and catastrophes of the plot, a deeper reversal is taking place in them all the time, so that the plot seems suddenly to be concerned with their own internal battles rather than the external adventures. More obviously with Edmund, who is tempted by the Witch with magic Turkish Delight and promises of power, falls, and betrays his brother and sisters, finds that sin brings nothing but frustration and bitterness, and struggles by way of repentance and suffering back ostensibly to where he was before but actually to a higher rung on the ladder of salvation, by virtue of his very fall and recovery. Less obviously with Eustace, whose badness is not spectacular, but who wins slowly out of it with the aid of all the adventures through which he passes.

Deepest of all, and not to be isolated or described, for it is a reflection rather than a substance, is the whole spiritual drama of Narnia, both in the doings of Aslan the great

Golden Lion and of all his people and of those whom he has called into Narnia from this other world of Man—of which Narnia is in some sort of a miniature likeness: an echo rather than a reproduction.

Though the penultimate volume, *The Magician's Nephew* (1955), tells of the events which went before it, the cycle begins with *The Lion, the Witch and the Wardrobe* (1950). Peter, Susan, Edmund and Lucy, four perfectly ordinary children, evacuated to Professor Kirke's big house in the country, discover that the Wardrobe in the Spare Room is at certain times the entrance to another world which they learn is called Narnia. Lucy enters first, and alone, meets Mr Tumnus the faun, and hears about the White Witch who rules the land with a rod of—ice: who has caused it to be 'always winter but never Christmas'. He is under orders to hand her over to the Witch, but thinks better of it and takes her back to the mysterious Lamp Post near which lies the way into the Wardrobe. No one believes Lucy's story; but Edmund by chance some days later makes his way into Narnia through the Wardrobe, meets the White Witch, decides to be on her side—and when he returns pretends that he still thinks there is no such place as Narnia and that Lucy is lying.

A little later, however, they all make their way into Narnia, find that Mr Tumnus's house has been wrecked by the Witch's Secret Police of wolves, and are entertained by the Beavers, who tell them that things are at last moving in Narnia, Aslan is about to return, and the prophecy is likely to be fulfilled that the Witch shall be overthrown when four Humans enter Narnia and sit on the four thrones in the Castle of Cair Paravel. Edmund slips away and tells the Witch, and there is an exciting chase across the frozen world where a great thaw suddenly sets in, to the Stone Table where Aslan will bring them to safety. The Witch, however, has Edmund, and prepares to sacrifice him so that the fourth throne can never be filled. But Aslan buys his life by giving his own. The Witch and her hideous satellites bind Aslan, insult him, spit on him, shave off his golden mane and tie him to the Stone Table where the Witch kills him. This lets loose the 'Deeper Magic from *before* the Dawn of Time'; Aslan is resurrected, and leads all Narnia that is loyal to him to the overthrow and destruction of the White Witch and her followers. Then Peter, Edmund, Susan and Lucy become Kings and Queens in Narnia, and reign for many years, until the White Stag leads them to the Lamp Post, and they come back through the Wardrobe—to find that no time at all has passed in this world, where they are once more the children who left it.

The following year (by human reckoning) the four children, while waiting on a station platform, are drawn suddenly into Narnia by a charm—and find themselves in the overgrown ruins which they at length learn are those of Cair Paravel. For in Narnia, many hundreds of years have passed. When they were in Narnia before, its only inhabitants were animals (mainly those who could talk) and such creatures as fauns, giants, dwarfs, naiads, unicorns and the like, but no humans. Now the human descendants of a crew of Earthly pirates have usurped the rule, and the Old People have gone into hiding. But Prince Caspian, who has blown the Magic Horn which drew them into Narnia, has revolted against his wicked uncle Miraz and the Old People have rallied round him; and the rest of the story tells of how Caspian conquered and brought peace and enlightenment to his country, in which Aslan was again known and loved.

The third book tells of how Edmund and Lucy, and their unpleasant cousin Eustace, who 'liked bossing and bullying',

and 'liked animals, especially beetles, if they were dead and
pinned on a card', and 'books if they were books of information', but 'never having read the right books, had no
idea how to tell a story straight', suddenly found themselves
on a ship the *Dawn Treader* which had just set sail from
Cair Paravel with Caspian in charge. Caspian is ostensibly
in search of the seven Narnian lords whom the wicked
Miraz had sent many years before to explore 'the unknown
Eastern Seas beyond the Lone Islands'; but,

'Why should we not come to the very eastern end of the
world? And what might we find there? I expect to find
Aslan's own country. It is always from the east, across the
sea, that the great Lion comes to us.'

The three children sail on this quest with Caspian and
Reepicheep the chivalrous Mouse, and meet many adventures. On one island Eustace is turned into a dragon, and is
only restored when he has learnt to value the friends whom
before he despised—and when Aslan has visited him. On
the Island of Voices they meet the Monopods, who have
been made invisible, but regain their visibility when Lucy
dares the adventure of the Magician's Book. They escape from
the Dark Island where dreams come true and nightmares
go on for ever; and come at last to 'The Beginning of End of
the World' where Ramandu, the Star King, and his daughter
preside over a table at which a great feast is spread daily
for the White Birds from Aslan's country—a mystic table,
since on it lies the Stone Knife with which Aslan was slain
by the White Witch: the Narnian equivalent, in fact, of the
Grail Castle. When at last the very End of the World is in
sight, only Edmund, Lucy, and Eustace go forward with
Reepicheep—though he alone is able to enter Aslan's
country. The children, learning that 'the door into Aslan's

country is from your own world . . . there is a way into my country from all the worlds', are sent home to look for it.

The Silver Chair (1953) jumps forward seventy years of Narnian time, though only a few months to Eustace, who is called into Narnia from his exceedingly unpleasant co-educational 'self-expression' school, in company with a chance school-acquaintance, Jill Pole. They meet Aslan on the brink of Narnia, and he tells them that they have been sent for to achieve a quest—that for the lost Prince Rilian, Caspian's son—and gives them certain instructions, the first of which they fail to carry out, since Eustace does not realise that the very ancient King whom he sees setting out for the World's End is Caspian, whom he left as a boy on the *Dawn Treader* apparently only a few months before. With the aid of the Owls they begin on their quest, and are guided by Puddleglum, who is a Marsh-wiggle, one of Lewis's most delightful creations, in appearance a very tall man, with a small body but excessively long arms and legs, and webbed fingers and toes, who always looks on the bright side of everything by ostentatiously expecting the worst. They are tempted aside into the Giant City, but escape and find the way down into the Underland where another Witch Queen is preparing to invade Narnia with an army of Earthmen—the subterranean gnomes whom she has en-slaved—and set Rilian on the throne as her puppet. He is under her spell for all but one hour of the twenty-four, during which he is bound in the Silver Chair as a madman. But, after a great scene of wizardry and temptation, the children and Puddleglum break the enchantment, the Witch turns into a serpent whom Rilian kills, and they escape out into Narnia in time for Rilian to bid farewell to Caspian, who has returned at Aslan's command in time to bless his son and die. In the epilogue in Aslan's country

Caspian, young and strong again, is allowed to step out into
the Human World for a few minutes to work Aslan's will
at the terrible school, before leaving Eustace and Jill, who
must live out their lives here before the final reunion in
Aslan's country.

The Silver Chair completes the cycle of closely connected
stories. *The Horse and his Boy* (1954), which was actually
written before it, is an isolated story, with purely Narnian
characters, set in the days described at the end of *The Lion,
the Witch and the Wardrobe*, when Peter was High King in
Cair Paravel. It tells how the boy Shasta of Calormen, a far
province of Narnia, runs away to avoid being sold as a slave,
and takes with him the Horse Bree, who turns out to be one
of the Talking Horses of Narnia—who, as we slowly discover, is really running away and taking Shasta with *him*.
They have many exciting adventures, and meet several old
friends including Mr Tumnus the Faun as well as Susan
and Edmund, before all ends happily with Shasta finding
his true father King Lune of Archenland and his brother
Prince Corin. And once again there are spiritual adventures
for Shasta and the Lady Aravis—as there are also for the
two Horses Bree and Hwin.

The two final stories, *The Magician's Nephew* (1955) and
The Last Battle (1956) form as it were the frame for the rest.
The first goes back to the very beginning of Narnia and
explains who the White Witch was and how she came to
power, why the Lamp Post stood where it did, and the
significance of the Wardrobe in Professor Kirke's Spare
Room. The children Polly and Digory see the ending of the
old world of Charn as well as the creation of the new world
of Narnia, and by the wicked magic of Digory's uncle Andrew and because he himself gives way to a temptation of
curiosity in Charn, the Witch, after a brief but tempestuous

visit to late Victorian London, gets into Narnia with the children just as Aslan is creating it. And it is Digory (who grows up to become Professor Kirke) who brings back the Magic Apple, from whose seeds grow the tree out of which the Wardrobe is made.

The last of all the stories tells of the final end of Narnia many centuries after any of the other stories when Aslan has long ceased to be seen walking visibly through his world, and the powers of evil are slowly undermining it. These are manifest in the neighbouring Calormenes who worship the devil Tash and in their tool the Ape Shift who dresses the simple, kindly Ass, Puzzle, in the skin of a lion and passes him off to the remnants of the Talking Beasts and the Dwarfs as Aslan himself, come again after many ages to rule with a sceptre of iron. Tirian, the last king of Narnia, falls into the power of the Calormenes who guard the stable where the false Aslan is kept, but on his prayer to the true Aslan he is rescued by Jill and Eustace, who come strangely into Narnia while on a train journey. They steal Puzzle from the stable, but the Calormenes (who have lost their faith, even in Tash) find to their terror that the monster Tash is actually there, and he carries off the Calormene leader and Shift. Tirian and his few faithful followers are defeated in the last battle and killed or driven into the stable. But those of them who enter it living find it the door into Aslan's country, and there those who are dead are waiting for them. Then Aslan himself comes to the door and holds his Last Judgement, calling in all those who are worthy, while the rest pass away into the darkness. This is followed by the complete destruction of Narnia, even to the stars falling from the sky and the sun being squeezed dry like an orange. Then those beyond the door follow Aslan up to the garden of paradise on the hilltop whence the White

Witch stole the Apple at the beginning of Narnia, and they are welcomed in by Reepicheep the Mouse, to find all the characters from the earlier books waiting there for them—and also Peter, Lucy, Edmund, Polly and Digory (Susan has renounced Narnia). For:

' "There *was* a real railway accident," said Aslan softly. "Your father and mother and all of you are—as you used to call it in the Shadowlands—dead. The term is over: the holidays have begun. The dream is ended: this is the morning." '

NOTE: Many readers have wondered whether Lewis had drawn out a scheme for the whole Narnian series before writing *The Lion, the Witch and the Wardrobe*: the answer, on the only reliable authority—his own—is that he had not. The earliest sketch for the first book was made in 1938; it was very different from the final version, and Aslan did not appear in it. After it had grown to its final form in 1949, the next few stories followed in natural sequence. Then Lewis turned back to seek for the origin of the Witch, the Wardrobe—and the Lamp Post. From this quest grew *The Magician's Nephew*, which ran away with its creator to make perhaps the most symmetrically perfect story of the series. In doing so, as careful readers will discover, the inspiration led Lewis to contradict one assumption or suggestion made in the two earliest stories, that there were no human beings from our world in Narnia before the children paid their first visit. (In the first draft of the story the 'Adam and Eve' of Narnia came from the lost world of Charn; both Lewis and a friend who read the manuscript agreed that these characters were unsatisfactory. In casting about for a replacement the cabman and his wife stepped suddenly and inevitably into their place—and were not to be ousted.)

IV. Aslan

'What you see and hear depends a good deal on where you are standing: it also depends on what sort of person you are.' In Narnia the wicked magician, Uncle Andrew, saw only wild animals roaring and trumpeting dangerously, while Polly and Digory saw Aslan choosing out the Talking Animals of Narnia and teaching them his wisdom. And this is also true of the Narnian books themselves.

From the start they have had some readers who can see little but harm and failure in them, and many more who have acclaimed them at once as outstanding works in the realm of children's literature, even as undoubted classics certain to take their place with the works of George MacDonald and E. Nesbit. And with children also the effect has been as varied, though again with a great majority of those who have sampled them coming for more and treasuring them among their supreme literary experiences. Consultation with junior librarians suggests that the majority of children who read of Narnia have a certain amount of literary background, and this is perhaps born out by the large sales which may point to the children who collect books for themselves.

Naturally an ordinary child's criticism or appreciation turns on the actual adventure, and it is not possible to discover the effect of the underlying allegory or moral inherent in all the stories. It certainly does not seem to put off any readers who are prepared to accept magic and the unknown at all. Judged simply as stories, for 'holding-value', *The Horse and his Boy* seems to be the most popular (perhaps also as combining in a completely novel way many of the delights of the 'pony book'), with *The Silver Chair* and *The Magician's Nephew* as good seconds. *Prince Caspian* appears to be the least popular, largely on account of the construction which prevents the story getting under way for a third of the book.

Adult criticism seems largely to have been shaped by disagreement or even disapproval of Lewis's views as they appear to the older reader at least; by the strange sentimentality which even now seems to get between an adult and his judgement where books for children are concerned; and by a sheer ignorance or perversity which cannot or will not understand what it is reading.

The first kind of criticism is easily understandable. Though the books may not have been attacked openly for the Christianity inherent in them, even in this present Age of Apostasy, many of the more summary and destructive criticisms probably stem from this.

'Dr Lewis's philosophy does not always bear analysis,' wrote the *Times Literary Supplement* reviewer of *The Last Battle*, 'his attitude, for instance, to "civilisation". The Ape desires "roads and big cities and schools and offices and whips and muzzles and saddles and cages and prisons— oh everything". Yet for Dr Lewis anarchy, the back-to-nature life, the rule of no-rule, is even more detestable.'* And: 'too often we find him bewitching himself with his own spells—above all with the spell of symbolic theology', wrote another reviewer, who also found in Lewis 'a kind of arrogance, even complacency . . . He enjoys the role of Aslan, as he enjoys receiving Aslan's admonition.'

This leads on to the sentimental critics who seem

---

* 'The critic means by *civilisation* things like big cities and offices. I mean things like justice, mercy, free speech, honour and courtesy. It is unfortunate that English uses the word in both senses.' C. S. L.

desperately afraid that the 'cruelty' and 'violence' of the books will hurt children, and cannot bear it that Lewis takes fairly unpleasant characters like Eustace and Jill at the beginning of *The Silver Chair*—even when so much of the point of the story is the development of their characters. 'Mr Lewis calls the boy and girl on whom his story depends (one can hardly describe them as hero and heroine) "Scrub" and "Pole". He makes them as unattractive as those names sound. They are poor, despicable creatures, serving as guinea pigs for the demonstration of an idea. The author displays their weaknesses, their shabby conduct, and exposes them to indignities without pity.' So the reviewer in *Junior Bookshelf*, who goes on to comment on 'that strange lack of tenderness which to my mind, weakens the effect and value of the work. It is striking in the descriptions of human character and behaviour, seeming to imply great contempt for the human race.'

Finally for sheer obtuseness the reader is hard to beat who found *The Lion, the Witch and the Wardrobe* confusing and occasionally cruel; and remarked that he preferred his fairy-tales to have a feeling of 'delicacy' and not to be concerned with real human beings.

If the last criticism needs answering, Lewis had already done so in the Preface to *That Hideous Strength*:

'If you ask why—intending to write about magicians, devils, pantomime, animals, and planetary angels—I nevertheless begin with such humdrum scenes and persons, I reply that I am following the traditional fairy-tale. We do not always notice its method, because the cottages, castles, wood-cutters and petty kings with which a fairy-tale opens have become for us as remote as the witches and ogres to which it proceeds. But they were not remote at all to the men who made and first enjoyed the stories.'

And Andrew Lang had done so even more explicitly in 1892 when pointing out in an article on 'Modern Fairy Stories' how badly the sentimental kind then being written departed from the whole point of the real tradition: 'In the old stories, despite the impossibility of the incidents, the interest is always real and human . . . The hero and heroine are persecuted or separated by cruel stepmothers or enchanters; they have wanderings and sorrows to suffer; they have adventures to achieve and difficulties to overcome. They must display courage, loyalty and address, courtesy, gentleness and gratitude. Thus they are living in a real human world, though it wears a mythical face, though there are giants and lions in the way. The old fairy-tales . . . unobtrusively teach the true lessons of our wayfaring in a world of perplexities and obstructions.'

A little more difficult to deal with are the allegations of 'cruelty' which will distress or frighten children—notably in the sacrifice of Aslan in *The Lion, the Witch and the Wardrobe*. 'There is a certain beauty even here for minds mature enough to accept it, but for young sensibilities I felt it beyond endurance,' wrote Eleanor Graham. 'The tension, the horror, the sheer pain is too great for young readers.'

It is such criticisms as this that Lewis is answering when he says: 'We do not know what will or will not frighten a child in this particular way. I say "in this particular way" for we must here make a distinction. Those who say that children must not be frightened may mean two things. They may mean (I) that we must not do anything likely to give the child those haunting, disabling, pathological fears against which ordinary courage is helpless: in fact *phobias*. His mind must, if possible, be kept clear of things he can't bear to think of. Or they may mean (II) that we must try to keep out of his mind the knowledge that he is born into a world of death, violence, wounds, adventure, heroism and cowardice, good and evil. If they mean the first I agree with them: but not if they mean the second. The second would indeed give children a false impression and feed them on escapism in the bad sense. There is something ludicrous in the idea of so educating a generation which is born to the Ogpu and the atomic bomb. Since it is so likely that they will meet cruel enemies, let them at least have heard of brave knights and heroic courage. Otherwise you are making destiny not brighter but darker. Nor do most of us find that violence and bloodshed in a story produce any haunting dread in the minds of children. As far as that goes, I side impenitently with the human race against the modern reformer. Let there be wicked kings and beheadings, battles and dungeons, giants and dragons, and let villains be soundly killed at the end of the book. Nothing will persuade me that this causes an ordinary child any kind of degree of fear beyond what it wants, and needs, to feel. For, of course, it wants to be a little frightened.

'The other fears—the phobias—are a different matter. I do not believe one can control them by literary means. We seem to bring them into the world with us ready made. No doubt the particular image on which a child's terror is fixed can sometimes be traced to a book. But is that the source, or the occasion, of the fear? If he had been spared that image, would not some other, quite unpredictable by you, have had the same effect? And I think it possible that by confining your child to blameless stories of child life in which nothing at all alarming ever happens, you would fail to banish the terrors, and would succeed in banishing all that can ennoble them or make them endurable. For in the fairy-tales, side by side with the terrible figures, we find the immemorial comforters and protectors, the radiant ones: and the terrible figures are not merely terrible, but sublime . . .'

It is perhaps worth mentioning that Mrs Molesworth, one of the writers of the most 'blameless stories of child life', having suffered from similar 'phobias' herself as a child, went out of her way to introduce her own and others into her books so as to lessen them or explain them away or guide towards a higher comfort children similarly inflicted.

The criticism of including in the Narnian stories things 'unsuitable for children' leads to the suggestion made by some critics that Lewis does not understand children and cannot draw them accurately or bring them to life. This is easier to understand, particularly when he is accused of modelling his children on those in E. Nesbit's books. For Lewis undoubtedly draws 'child' in the general from the child he knew best—himself: his extremely retentive memory of the feelings, experiences and thoughts of that childhood is shown in *Surprised by Joy* (1955).* For the Narnian stories were not told to actual children; nor had he any but the most superficial acquaintance with the species at the time of writing. All the stories were completed before his brief and intensely happy marriage left him a widower with two stepsons nearing the end of their prep school days. So that the externals of childhood may have been seen to some extent 'through the spectacles of books' (in which naturally E. Nesbit was the most useful), and some of them grafted on to the recollections of his own

---

* Lewis told me definitely that none of the characters or adventures in the Narnia stories are drawn from the Animal Land of his childhood inventions. The whole spirit of Narnia is different, as he points out in *Surprised by Joy*: 'Animal Land had nothing whatever in common with Narnia except the anthropomorphic beasts. Animal Land, by its whole quality, excluded the least hint of wonder.'

childhood days, and the child friends and acquaintances of the actual period when Nesbit was writing. This explains why the most completely successful and four dimensional children in his books are Polly and Digory in *The Magician's Nephew*, set (so far as Earthly time is concerned) in the days when 'Mr Sherlock Holmes was still living in Baker Street and the Bastables were looking for treasure in the Lewisham Road'. After them come the completely Narnian children who were never in the human world; Shasta in *The Horse and his Boy* and Prince Caspian (though he is more lightly sketched as he is seldom the centre of the picture). Of Eustace (in *The Voyage of the 'Dawn Treader'* and *The Silver Chair*) it is harder to speak, since as adult readers we are more interested in his spiritual development; but his external characteristics do seem completely credible and true to life. Polly, again, is more shadowy and lightly drawn, as is Susan; but Lucy comes through as a full person in her own right, and would be recognisable at once if we met her.

The adult characters are of much less importance, except in *The Magician's Nephew*, where Uncle Andrew is perhaps slightly caricatured though still acceptable, and Frank the cabby is a beautiful little miniature of simple goodness. The Narnian Kings and Calormenes are much more shadowy: Rilian and Tirian are less distinct than Caspian, and the rest loom a little larger than life in the bewildering mist with its stirring background of music that is our general vision of Narnia.

Out of that mist come character after character for magic moments of their own, gleaming suddenly into life in the midst of an incident and then fading once more into the moving pageant of the background: Mr Tumnus the Faun, a bear or two, the beavers and the badgers, Puzzle the Donkey, the horses Bree and Hwin and, in his own dimensions, Strawberry the cab horse who became Fledge the Hippogryph, and so to the most fully created of them all Puddleglum the Marsh-wiggle and Reepicheep the wonderful Talking Mouse who by the end claims perhaps the highest place in our affections.

The sense of wonder and discovery, the feeling of awakened memory rather than of cunningly drawn mind-pictures, is helped greatly by the descriptions of scenery and of even the smallest facet of nature—always growing naturally out of the narrative and never superimposed. Lewis's long, solitary walks in Ulster and Surrey, and in the country round Oxford have borne good fruit in these vivid composite scenes: the love of all the beauties of scenery and nature, flora and fauna, go to their creation—from the mountains of Donegal—'as near heaven as you can get in Thulcandra'—to the apparently instinctive sympathy with mice or badgers or bears.

In the Narnian stories there is nearly always the curious feeling of the personal experience. Lewis knew ships well from his many crossings over the Irish Sea, and harbours from Belfast and Liverpool: but the *Dawn Treader* is a real galley and not a ferryboat with poop and sails stuck on. Real warfare he knew also, perhaps even hand-to-hand fighting, from the Great War—but hardly with sword and scimitar, longbow and battle-axe: yet there is never a feeling that these have been 'got up' from encyclopedias or reproduced from literary sources.

'I see pictures.' This, on the outer layer at least, is the nearest we can get to explaining the vivid and effective quality of the Narnian books: this, and Lewis's supreme skill in making us see the pictures too. But 'there are gaps. Then at last you have to do some deliberate thinking.' This also explains the occasional weaknesses, the slightly episodic nature of the earlier books, and the brilliant scenes and incidents which occasionally hang together rather than growing out of each other.

There is just a suspicion of this even in *Perelandra*. It is most apparent in *The Lion, the Witch and the Wardrobe*, though the general suspense and the steady heightening of interest and expectancy prevents it from breaking the 'glamour' for the child reader, though the critical adult cannot help feeling from time to time: 'Here are superb incidents, vivid moments, thought-provoking ideas—but they have come separately and been fitted together: oh, so cunningly—but there *is* a trace of the cement.' *Prince Caspian* by the nature of its construction seems less contrived in this way; and *The Voyage of the 'Dawn Treader'* triumphs completely since it is intended to consist of consecutive adventures as the ship sails among unknown islands towards the World's End—and some of the separate incidents in their settings are among the best and most memorable in the whole series.

The Horse and his Boy combines the picaresque with the plot pleasantly and excitingly, but less memorably. Only with *The Silver Chair* does Lewis come fully into his kingdom—or into all the provinces of his kingdom—both constructing a complete and single unity with each incident growing naturally as part of the whole, and conjuring up the characters, strange or ordinary, against marvellous and unexpected backgrounds, as if the circumstances and not the author had called them into being. *The Magician's Nephew* is just as perfect a unity and as rounded and satisfying an experience, and it is very much a matter of opinion whether it or *The Silver Chair* is the best of the series: Marcus Crouch finds the Nesbit influence too much in evidence, another critic finds additional compulsion in precisely this familiar echo caught and developed from the original tinkling melody into a great opera.

There is no slackening of power in *The Last Battle*, but its nature does not demand an involved plot; the great movement is as of a slowly rising wave or the final surge of the music rising to a solemn climax and fading away into a hushed and awe-filled silence.

Here we come nearest to the deep core of the stories: the moral, or the religious truth which is, in the highest sense, their inspiration.

'Let the pictures tell you their own moral,' said Lewis. 'For the moral inherent in them will rise from whatever spiritual roots you have succeeded in striking during the whole course of your life . . . Everything in the story should arise from the whole cast of the author's mind. We must write for children out of those elements in our own imagination which we share with children: differing from our child readers not by any less, or less serious, interest in the things we handle, but by the fact that we have other interests which children would not share with us. The matter of our story should be part of the habitual furniture of our minds . . . We must meet children as equals in that area of our nature where we are their equals. Our superiority consists partly in commanding other areas, and partly (which is more relevant) in the fact that we are better at telling stories than they are. The child as reader is neither to be patronised nor idolised: we talk to him as man to man.' ['I am almost inclined to set it up as a canon that a children's story which is enjoyed only by children is a bad children's story. The good ones last,' Lewis had already said.] 'But the worst attitude of all would be the professional attitude which regards children in the lump as a sort of raw material which we have to handle. We must of course try to do them no harm! we may under the Omnipotence, sometimes dare to hope that we may do them good. But only such good as involves treating them with respect. We must not imagine that we are Providence or Destiny.'

The truest, the unique strength of the Chronicles of Narnia, the spirit incarnating them, the breath of Aslan which gives them life so that they will, I believe, live to take their permanent place among the great works of children's literature, is 'the whole cast of the author's mind' which has gone into their making. The mind of a true scholar, of one of the best-read men of his age; of a superb craftsman in the art of letters, with a gift for story-telling; of a thinker, logician and theologian who has plumbed the depths of the dark void of atheism and come by the hardest route on his pilgrimage back to God.

In Aslan's farewell to Edmund and Lucy at the end of *The Voyage of the 'Dawn Treader'* we have the whole theme and inspiration of Narnia:

' "Dearest," said Aslan very gently, "you and your brother will never come back to Narnia."

"Oh, *Aslan*!!" said Edmund and Lucy both together in despairing voices.

"You are too old, children," said Aslan, "and you must begin to come close to your own world now."

"It isn't Narnia, you know," sobbed Lucy. "It's *you*. We shan't meet *you* there. And how can we live, never meeting you?"

"But you shall meet me, dear one," said Aslan.

"Are—are you there too, Sir?" said Edmund.

"I am," said Aslan. "But there I have another name. You must learn to know me by that name. This was the very reason why you were brought to Narnia, that by knowing me here for a little, you may know me better there." '

C. S. Lewis Book List

I. THE CHRONICLES OF NARNIA

The Lion, the Witch and the Wardrobe Illustrated by Pauline Baynes. Geoffrey Bles, 1950

Prince Caspian. The Return to Narnia Illustrated by Pauline Baynes. Geoffrey Bles, 1951

The Voyage of the 'Dawn Treader' Illustrated by Pauline Baynes. Geoffrey Bles, 1952

The Silver Chair Illustrated by Pauline Baynes. Geoffrey Bles, 1953

The Horse and his Boy Illustrated by Pauline Baynes. Geoffrey Bles, 1954

The Magician's Nephew Illustrated by Pauline Baynes. The Bodley Head, 1955

The Last Battle Illustrated by Pauline Baynes. The Bodley Head, 1956

All the above are published in the United States by the Macmillan Company, and most of them have been translated into numerous languages. *The Last Battle* was awarded the Carnegie Medal in 1956

All have been issued in Puffin Books

II. ROMANCES

Out of the Silent Planet. The Bodley Head, 1938
Perelandra. The Bodley Head, 1943
That Hideous Strength. The Bodley Head, 1945
Till We have Faces. Geoffrey Bles, 1956

III. OTHER BOOKS

Spirits in Bondage : A Cycle of Lyrics By Clive Hamilton. Heinemann, 1919

Dymer By Clive Hamilton. J. M. Dent, 1926. (With a new Preface, 1950)

The Pilgrim's Regress. J. M. Dent, 1933. (Revised edition, with new Preface, Geoffrey Bles, 1943)

The Allegory of Love. Oxford University Press, 1936

Rehabilitations, and Other Essays. Oxford University Press, 1939

The Personal Heresy (With E. M. W. Tillyard). Oxford University Press, 1939

The Problem of Pain. Geoffrey Bles, 1940

The Screwtape Letters. Geoffrey Bles, 1942. (With *Screwtape Proposes a Toast*, and a new Preface, 1961)

Broadcast Talks. Geoffrey Bles, 1942

A Preface to Paradise Lost. Oxford University Press, 1942

Christian Behaviour. Geoffrey Bles, 1943

The Abolition of Man. Oxford University Press, 1943. (Reprinted by Geoffrey Bles)

Beyond Personality. Geoffrey Bles, 1944

The Great Divorce. Geoffrey Bles, 1945

Miracles. Geoffrey Bles, 1947

Arthurian Torso (With Charles Williams). Oxford University Press, 1948

Transposition, and other Addresses. Geoffrey Bles, 1949

Mere Christianity. Geoffrey Bles, 1952

English Literature in the Sixteenth Century, excluding Drama (The Oxford History of English Literature, Vol III). Oxford University Press, 1954

Surprised by Joy : The Shape of My Early Life. Geoffrey Bles, 1955

Reflections on the Psalms. Geoffrey Bles, 1958

The Four Loves. Geoffrey Bles, 1960

The World's Last Night, and other Essays. Harcourt, Brace (N.Y.), 1960

Studies in Words. Cambridge University Press, 1960 (enlarged edition 1967)

An Experiment in Criticism. Cambridge University Press, 1961

A Grief Observed. 'By N. W. Clerk', Faber, 1961

They Asked for a Paper. Geoffrey Bles, 1962

Letters to Malcolm : Chiefly on Prayer. Geoffrey Bles, 1964

The Discarded Image. Cambridge University Press, 1964

Poems (Edited by Walter Hooper). Geoffrey Bles, 1964

Screwtape Proposes a Toast, and Other Pieces. Collins, 1965

Studies in Medieval and Renaissance Literature (Edited by Walter Hooper). Cambridge University Press, 1966

Letters of C. S. Lewis (Edited by W. H. Lewis). Geoffrey Bles, 1966

Of Other Worlds : Essays and Stories (Edited by Walter Hooper). Geoffrey Bles, 1966

Christian Reflections (Edited by Walter Hooper). Geoffrey Bles, 1967

Spenser's Images of Life (Edited by Alastair Fowler). Cambridge University Press, 1967

Letters to An American Lady (Edited by Clyde S. Kilby). William B. Eerdmans, U.S.A., 1967

Literary Essays (Edited by Walter Hooper). Cambridge University Press, 1969

IV. PAMPHLETS AND ESSAYS OF PARTICULAR INTEREST

**Hamlet, the Prince or the Poem?* Oxford University Press, 1942

George MacDonald : An Anthology. Geoffrey Bles, 1946

†'On Stories' In *Essays Presented to Charles Williams.* Oxford University Press, 1947

Introduction to J. B. Phillips: *Letters to Young Churches.* Geoffrey Bles, 1947

Vivisection. National Anti-Vivisection Society, 1948

*'Kipling's World' In *Literature and Life.* Harrap & Co., 1948

**The Literary Impact of the Authorised Version.* Athlone Press, 1950

Hero and Leander. Oxford University Press, 1952

†'On Three Ways of Writing for Children' In *Proceedings of the Annual Conference*, The Library Association, 1952. (Delivered at Bournemouth, 29 April 1952)

**De Descriptione Temporum.* Cambridge University Press, 1955.

Shall We Lose God in Outer Space? S.P.C.K., 1959

'Haggard Rides Again' *Time and Tide*, September 3, 1960

* These four essays were included in *They Asked for a Paper* in 1962
† The two essays were included in *Of Other Worlds* in 1966

V. WRITINGS ABOUT C. S. LEWIS

Chad Walsh: *C. S. Lewis : Apostle to the Skeptics.* The Macmillan Company, New York, 1949 (Not published in England)

C. S. Lewis: *Surprised by Joy: The Shape of My Early Life.* Geoffrey Bles, 1955

Roger Lancelyn Green: *Tellers of Tales* (Revised edition). Edmund Ward, 1953 (Rewritten edition 1965)

Marcus S. Crouch: 'Chronicles of Narnia' *The Junior Bookshelf:* Vol XX. No. 5. November 1956

Chosen for Children. The Library Association, 1957

Roger Lancelyn Green: *Into Other Worlds: Space-Flight in Fiction from Lucian to Lewis.* Abelard-Schuman, 1957

Charles Moorman: *Arthurian Triptych: Mythic Materials in Charles Williams, C. S. Lewis and T. S. Eliot.* California University Press (and C.U.P.), 1960

Margery Fisher: *Intent upon Reading.* Brockhampton Press, 1961

Marcus S. Crouch: *Treasure Seekers and Borrowers.* The Library Association, 1962

Clyde S. Kilby: *The Christian World of C. S. Lewis* (Michigan, U.S.A.), 1964. Marcham Manor Press, 1965

Jocelyn Gibb (Editor): Light on C. S. Lewis, 1966 (Essays by nine writers)

Beatrix Potter

MARCUS CROUCH

CONTENTS

L

ACKNOWLEDGMENTS

There have been four stages in the appreciation of Beatrix Potter. Until 1946 only the small circle of the author's friends and relatives knew more than was represented by the published books. Miss Margaret Lane's *Tale of Beatrix Potter* published in that year showed, with tenderness and humour, what kind of person the creator of Peter Rabbit had been. *The Art of Beatrix Potter*, in 1955, revealed the range and power of her work in colour and line as well as her long and patient apprenticeship in art. The publication of the transcribed Journals in 1966 showed how, during the critical years of her development, she trained herself in observation and in command of a flexible and sensitive prose style. A second edition of Miss Lane's *Tale* in 1968 corrected some impressions in the light of the Journals. Grateful thanks are due to the publishers, Frederick Warne & Co. Ltd, for permission to quote freely from all these sources and to *Junior Bookshelf* for permission to reprint (as chapter III) an article I wrote for that journal in August 1966.

Mr Leslie Linder, whose knowledge of Beatrix Potter's work is as full as his love for it is deep, made me free of his collection of original paintings, letters and personalia, and let me read his transcriptions from the Journals. For much delight and help I am deeply grateful.

My thanks go also to Dr Otto J. Shaw for letting me examine his collection of original editions of Beatrix Potter's books.

Lastly I am grateful to many friends overseas who have written to tell me of the joy which these books give to children of many different races, creeds and traditions.

1. Introductory

The scene is a small library in Kent. Among the people crowding in is a woman accompanied by her daughter, a minute scrap of a child not yet four. Mother turns left into the adult library; Jill, silent and self-contained, marches into the children's room, goes at once to a shelf, takes down a book, and settles herself at a table to read. The book is *The Tale of Pigling Bland* and, oblivious to the noise around her —for the room is full of lively children—she is deeply engrossed in the story.

It will be perhaps two years before Jill can read, in the school sense; but for a year she has known the Beatrix Potter stories and, with her mother's help, has entered the enchanted world of the imagination, seeing through inspired eyes the beauty of everyday things and learning to savour the shape and sound of fine words. Now she can 'read'; that is, she realises that there is a relationship between the pictures and the mysterious black characters that match them. Some of the symbols are beginning, like royal cartouches to the early Egyptologists, to look familiar. Before long they will become words.

Jill is a symbol of the perennial miracle of Beatrix Potter. Several generations have come under her spell. It would be a bold man who would put a term to her influence. She was 'old-fashioned' in her own day. Today her work is timeless, seemingly indestructible. There will always be Jills to enjoy, in her company, the fun, the sturdy common sense, the vision.

Beatrix Potter would be the last person to tolerate this

present study of her work. 'Great rubbish, absolute bosh!' was her description of an appreciative article which someone was ill-advised enough to show her. She had a strong dislike for such 'silliness' and a sharp way with admirers from her own country. With Americans she was more at ease and accepted their homage graciously. Writers, however, are not always sound critics of their own work, and generations of readers will continue to marvel at the quality of her work, regardless of her own self-evaluation. I am attempting, therefore, to set down here a little of what her books have meant to children, who in her company have learnt to laugh, to observe, to share vicariously in the creation of character and the shaping of words.

11. A Quiet Life?

Beatrix Potter was born on July 28, 1866, at Bolton Gardens, Kensington. Born at the height of the Victorian age, she came from a characteristic Victorian family of the moneyed middle-class. The Potters had made a fortune in the Lancashire textile industry, but Beatrix's parents were of the generation which spent, rather than made, the money. From her family, and particularly from her mother's side of the family, the sturdy individual Cromptons, she derived her obstinacy, her aggressive lack of sentimentality. In later life she wrote briefly of her 'tough ancestry', and it was this which helped her to resist stubbornly when the dead hand of a rigid social code seemed likely to keep her from the fulfilment of her destiny.

Miss Lane has described the monotony of her life at home. Unquestionably it was dull; in other circumstances she might more readily have discovered her talents. It was perhaps not much duller than that of other Victorian households, except that the Potters were less prolific than most families and Beatrix had the company only of a younger brother, Bertram. There were the visitors. Mr Potter was wealthy, leisured and a skilled photographer; he had the acquaintance of many important men of his day. Victorian children were seen and not heard, but they could see; and Beatrix had opportunity to develop that power of observation which helped to make her a writer, in the company of the kindly, the pompous, the foolish.

Then there were the holidays. The Potters took their social habits with them, and no doubt the daily round was much the same in Scotland, Wales and the Lakes as it was at Bolton Gardens; but there was the scenery and the company, unauthorised perhaps, of country people—with the young child's ear keenly aware of the strange cadences of dialect. There were animals to be seen, pets to be acquired and carried about—surely a triumph of the Potter (or Crompton) obstinacy—from household to household. Not every child was allowed, or at least not actively forbidden, to keep mice, hedgehogs, snails and minnows.

Bertram went away to Charterhouse; Beatrix was growing up. The pretty, solemn child became a rather old-fashioned, odd girl. Her earliest dated drawings showed a distinct but unexceptional talent. She was clearly capable of using her eyes and putting on paper what she saw in fine detail. Her many visits to the museums at South Kensington were training her to an appreciation of form and to habits of scientific objectivity. Quite suddenly she was no longer a skilled copier, but a selector of significant detail. Her paintings of flowers and fungi were accurate and aesthetically satisfying.

The fungus paintings had to wait until 1967 to reach a wide audience. They were the direct inspiration of Dr W. P. K. Findlay's *Wayside and woodland fungi*, published by Warne in that year, in which sixty-one of them appeared for the first time in an appropriate context.

From 1881 to 1897, that is between the ages of fifteen and thirty, Beatrix kept a journal. In 1946 Miss Lane wrote of this period, 'almost nothing is known about it, for the apparently sufficient reason that there is nothing to know'.* For many years after the publication of Miss Lane's *Tale*, Leslie Linder worked on these journals (now in the possession of the National Trust), broke the cipher they were

* *Tale of Beatrix Potter*, p. 49.

written in, and discovered the daily thoughts and activities of the writer. The journals are remarkable documents. Written in a complicated code, they have clearly, from the evidence of the fluent calligraphy, been written down at high speed. The writer must indeed have *thought* in this private language. The contents reveal a life, quiet perhaps, but full of interest for the intelligent young woman. There were people to meet, devastating judgments to be made, everyday things to do. Whatever frustrations Beatrix suffered at this time, she certainly was not bored. The journals reveal, too, that here was a writer in the making. The shrewd observations are recorded in a clean, lively prose, written without pretensions (for these words were for the writer alone) but with craftsmanship. A fuller examination of the Journals is included in Chapter III.

During this period, perhaps when she was making her earliest tentative imaginative drawings in the Caldecott manner, she met her first influential friend. This was Canon Rawnsley, the Vicar of Wray, where the Potters rented a mock-baronial castle. Canon Rawnsley, soon to be co-founder of the National Trust, was all that the Potters were not: an enthusiast, an exuberant and tireless worker, a live person, interested in people. Through contact with him Beatrix Potter began to learn for the first time that life could be lived more abundantly beyond the circle of home and family. Important too at this time was Bertram Potter's decision to become an artist; some of the glamour of this decision surely rubbed off on to his sister.

Somewhere about this time, before 1893, Beatrix Potter's first published work appeared. This was a set of pictures, in colour, to illustrate some indifferent verses by Frederic E. Weatherly, *A Happy Pair*, which was printed in Germany. One of the pictures is reproduced in *The Art of Beatrix*

Potter (p. 155). The work is not of intrinsic quality, but it is interesting to note the treatment of animal characters, one of whom is Benjamin Bunny.

At the same time Beatrix Potter was experimenting further with designs for book illustrations, and a series of pencil drawings for *Uncle Remus* have survived. There was something of Walter Crane here in the use of picture-frames and marginal decoration; the drawing of animals, however, was individual. The artist was already an expert in rabbits.

From the nineties date many of the picture-letters, mostly written to members of the family of Annie Carter, who had been Beatrix Potter's governess and was now a Mrs Moore living with her children in Wandsworth. From Bolton Gardens, or from one of the many holiday houses, letters came to Noël Moore and his sisters containing gossip of everyday affairs and sharply characteristic tales of animals. One of these little letters, which began abruptly, 'I don't know what to write to you, so I shall tell you a story about four little rabbits, whose names were Flopsy, Mopsy, Cottontail and Peter', she borrowed from Noël some years later. Rewritten and with extra pictures it looked quite like a little book, so she sent if off to Frederick Warne & Co. It came back with a courteous rejection. After several similar experiences, she decided on a private edition. The modest success of this was encouragement to Warne's to look at the book again, and they accepted it for publication after substantial revision and with coloured illustrations. *Peter Rabbit* had begun the career which was to take him into most of the countries of the world and into the lives of innumerable children. The author was thirty-six.

The story of the next ten years is one of many books, of battles with the family, of adventure, frustration and tragedy. The first friendship brought to her by her books was that of Norman Warne, the youngest member of the publishing house, who quickly appreciated her quality as a writer and as a person. His patience and interest were inexhaustible, and she discussed with him the minute details of each book. Their friendship was as strong as it was quiet. It could hardly have surprised anyone, although it annoyed the Potters greatly, when in 1905 they became engaged. A family battle followed which ended only when Norman died suddenly at the end of the year.

The tragedy would have been even harder to bear had it not been for the adventure. Beatrix Potter had made a modest sum out of her books, and this, with a legacy, she invested in the purchase of a Lakeland farm—surely an extraordinarily bold step for an Edwardian spinster of the middle class. Hill Top Farm was in Sawrey, near the borders of Lancashire and Westmorland, a village she had visited often during the family holidays. She loved the country and spoke the language of the people. Now she owned a small part of it. She established the sitting tenant as her foreman, and whenever family affairs permitted she went to her farm, supervising improvements to the buildings, battling with workmen, watching the growth of stock, energetically exterminating rats. The London-born girl was a countrywoman by instinct and ancestry; she was a shrewd farmer as well as business-woman, and gradually extended her hold on the village until she owned a great part of it.

Her legal business at Sawrey was handled by a country lawyer, Mr William Heelis, of Hawkshead. Temperamentally they were complementary, and he proved to be a kindly, sympathetic companion. In 1913 he proposed marriage to her. Once again weary battle was joined with her parents, but in October they were married at St Mary Abbot's in

Kensington. Beatrix Potter was then forty-seven. Mr and Mrs Heelis set up home at Castle Farm, Sawrey.

For Beatrix Potter, more than most women, marriage marked the end of one life and the beginning of another. After a lifetime of subordinating her wishes to those of her parents, she was free to live where she wished and, with a reasonable sufficiency of means, to do very much what she wanted. It is not really surprising that Mrs Heelis of Sawrey turned away from Miss Potter's successes as an author and artist. For the thirty years of her married life, although she took pleasure in the admiration, and the occasional visits, of American friends, and continued to enjoy the friendship of individual children, she wrote only occasionally and reluctantly, and instead devoted her considerable energies to the activities of a working countrywoman. She discouraged in the most brusque way, the advances of English admirers of her work. Clearly she considered—and who shall say that she was wrong?—that raising pedigree Herdwick sheep was a more useful occupation than making picture-books. For her it was undoubtedly a happier occupation.

There is little more to be said. Happiness is uneventful, and the long, hard-working, deeply satisfying days passed without major disturbance. Mr Potter died, Bertram died, Mrs Potter and all her Bolton Gardens impedimenta were translated to Windermere, more land was bought. Mrs Heelis became an expert sheep farmer, knowing her own as she had known so many animals in the past, relishing the company and speech of shepherds and fellow farmers. Her adventurous buying of land and property continued, and had effects by which everyone benefits today. Through Canon Rawnsley she had been interested from the beginning in the work of the National Trust. Now she saw the need of that work for the protection of the unique character of the

Lake District, and by discreet purchase and careful husbandry she prevented the spoliation of the country she loved in so practical a way. Several thousands of acres, mostly in the Coniston, Eskdale, Hawkshead and Troutbreck areas, came to the Trust by Mrs Heelis's will. She was moreover a prime mover in the many public subscriptions by which much more incomparable country was saved for ever. One of her smaller bequests, but for all lovers of her work a gift beyond price, was the 201 acres in Sawrey including Hill Top itself with all its furniture, pictures, china and other personalia.

Delmar Banner's portrait (which hangs in the National Portrait Gallery) belongs to this period. This shows surely the Mrs Heelis she had chosen to be, kindly but shrewd and where necessary ruthless, a good friend and a formidable opponent. Dressed in her best, she carries an umbrella and, one would guess, a sale catalogue. Behind her is a glimpse of the hills and her Herdwick sheep.

Illness and the coming of war made her last years painful and troubled, but did not damage her spirit. She died, seventy-seven years old, on December 22, 1943, with courage undiminished, as prickly and eccentric as ever.

III. A Secret Apprenticeship

'Almost nothing is known about it' (the period from her seventeenth to her twenty-seventh year) 'for the apparently sufficient reason that there is nothing to know.' Thus Margaret Lane in 1946. Twenty years later, through the extraordinary industry and dedication of Leslie Linder, the most minute details of Beatrix Potter's life during the years of her growth to maturity became known.

Beatrix Potter kept a journal intermittently for sixteen years. She wrote it in a self-invented code, at first briefly and precisely, later with quite amazing fluency. (One of the marvels revealed by this transcript is the mind which could pour out thoughts, facts and ideas with such prodigality, all, in effect, in a strange language.) The journals went, with much of her property, into the care of the National Trust and from them on loan to that arch-Potterian Leslie Linder. By a combination of chance and hard work Mr Linder found the clue to the secret of her code, and his years of labour were crowned in the centenary year of the author by the publication of the transcribed journal, which afforded a unique view into the mind of a most remarkable and versatile woman.

For the second time, lovers of Beatrix Potter's books owed a debt to Mr Linder, who in 1955 was the prime mover in the publication of *The Art of Beatrix Potter*. This book revealed that behind the spring-like freshness of the pictures in these incomparable books lay years of patient observation and practice in an art, the mastery of which did not come easily. In the Journals readers were privileged to see the artist at work in her other medium, practising and refining her craft of words, so that in the end she was writing for her private satisfaction, with a fluency and power which any professional writer might envy. It has always been clear that the text of her books was flawless in its distilled simplicity. The writer who achieved perfection in the thousand words of *Peter Rabbit* had undertaken a voluntary apprenticeship in her art, of which the Journals are evidence.

The transcribed journals occupy 438 pages of print, a very long book indeed. Are they worth reading? Anyone who loves the Beatrix Potter books, or who has been fascinated and unsatisfied by the picture of the author contained in Margaret Lane's *Tale of Beatrix Potter*, or who is interested in the social history of late Victorian England, must answer 'Yes.' The Journals are not merely a remarkable survival; they are the door to a remarkable mind.

At first the fifteen-year-old writer is concerned largely with trivia, everyday events, jokes, scraps of information. 'Miss Ellen Terry's complexion is made of such an expensive enamel that she can only afford to wash her face once a fortnight.' Very early on she shows a gift for visual characterisation. A Devon landlady is 'a tiny little old woman, humpbacked and energetic, slumping about at a great rate.' She is never, as one might have feared from her biography, bored. Life is full of interesting things to see and do. Above all, there are pictures. The young Beatrix Potter sees herself, and occasionally dares to admit as much in her secret writing, as a painter. A painting by Angelica Kauffmann, in 1883, 'shows what a woman has done' and, by implication, what another woman may do. She is a sharp critic of art, undeterred by the high repute of painters whom she does not admire. Very gradually her passionate concern with painting is ousted by an interest in science, geology and botany, and the last pages reflect her growing confidence in her study of fungi. The last entry, dated early in 1897, deals with the paper which she has prepared for presentation to the Linnean Society. Why did she write no more? And why did she withdraw her paper from publication in the Society's Proceedings? Revealing as the Journals are, the enigma of Beatrix Potter remains.

The Journals nevertheless offer a solution to one mystery. How did the shy, unhappy child of Bolton Gardens become the strong-minded eccentric Mrs Heelis of Sawrey and Troutbeck Park? In the Journals we see that eccentric in the making. The tough Lancashire Potter (or rather Crompton) is evident in innumerable entries. She shows for her father a tolerant affection far from the awed respect of the average middle-class Victorian for an august papa. 'If my papa has a fault, he is rather voluble in conversation and ...oppressively well informed,' she wrote in 1892, and earlier she made fun of his naïve enthusiasm for sailing.

Through her father, and the family friend Millais, she knew many public figures and held strong views about them. John Bright comes off well, but Gladstone—'the old rogue' —is invariably treated roughly. There is a brilliant description of him at the Royal Academy of 1890. In 1892 he is 'transparently dishonest,' and at the death of Tennyson she exclaims, 'What a pity it was not Mr Gladstone.' Her political opinions are uncompromising.

Although she speaks to herself, touchingly, as having 'lived so much asleep and out of life,' and indeed the Journals are a record of recurrent ill-health, there is little here to suggest a frustrated life. Here is a woman of wide-ranging mind, interested in a vast world of subjects, and largely—bearing in mind the inhibitions of her time—able to pursue them. Not unexpectedly she shows a deep love and understanding of nature, and occasionally writes most beautifully about the visual world: 'There is sometimes a solitary robin haunting the dwarfed thorns, and nearly always an uncanny blue hare on the lone hearth stone,' written of a deserted Scottish village. But this is no sentimentalist, escaping from the harshness of life into Nature. Not only does she see the natural world with clear, unclouded vision, she delights in people of all kinds and classes, and shows a most unexpected liking for machinery. 'To my mind there is scarcely a more splendid beast in the world than a large Locomotive.'

Appropriately the Journals rise to their finest heights towards the close, when the writer, after her first stay in the village of Sawrey which was to become her beloved home and the setting of her best books, sums up from her London house her impressions of the North country, playing more than half seriously with fantasies of the fungi which were the subject of her most scientific study. Out of this fantasy comes the thought: 'What heaven can be more real than to retain the spirit-world of childhood tempered and balanced by knowledge and common-sense, to fear no longer the terror that flieth by night, yet to feel truly and understand a little, a very little, of the story of life.' At thirty, and with her life's-work not yet begun, Beatrix Potter miraculously sums up the essential quality of her books: 'the spirit-world of childhood, tempered and balanced by common-sense.'

It is a richly rewarding experience to read these Journals, to enter, with respect and affection, the mind of a most remarkable woman. A good artist is more than the sum-total of his achievements. The Journals provide a clue to the nature of Beatrix Potter, who gave us the finest picture-stories in our heritage, who became a successful farmer, and who bequeathed to the nation some of the finest landscapes of the Lake country, who thus lived three fruitful and satisfying lives, but who was herself bigger than the sum-total of her achievements.

IV. Bibliographical

For a number of years Beatrix Potter has had the attention of book collectors. She was, from the earliest days, extremely popular and succeeding generations of children have worn her books to pieces. Early editions in really good condition are consequently hard to come by and have the collector's virtue of rarity. For some indeed—the three painting books—rarity is almost their principal virtue. Moreover the bibliographical history of these early editions is complex. They were published in a number of different bindings, issues were not always dated, and copies abound in problems which are at once the bibliographer's despair and delight.

In 1954 Jane Quinby published her *Bibliographical Check List**. This is based on a number of collections, public and private, in the United States, notably that of the late Urling S. Iselin, and lists thirty titles and no less than 109 differing versions. Miss Quinby admits, 'It may be some time before a definitive bibliography of the works . . . is completed', and her work is clearly incomplete. Collectors who use this check list—and it is indispensable—will find many problems still unsolved, and this in itself is enough to ensure that bibliophiles will continue to be exercised over the colour of the original boards of *The Pie and the Patty-Pan* or the advertisements in the second edition of *The Story of a Fierce Bad Rabbit*.

An article by Laurie Deval in the *Book Collector* (Winter 1966) takes a closer look at some of the bibliographical

* Quinby, Jane. *Beatrix Potter. A bibliographical check list.* New York, 1954.

eccentricities of the books. This was prompted by the magnificent centenary exhibition staged at the National Book League in that year.

Textual and typographical details, interesting as they are, will not much concern the majority of those who come to these little books for the delight of their literary and artistic style. I have however commented, in the appreciations of individual books, on the main points of bibliographical interest, particularly those which seem to reveal the improving hand of the artist.

v. The works—in the beginning

The Tale of Peter Rabbit had its origin in a picture-letter sent from Scotland to Noël Moore, the son of Beatrix Potter's former governess, in 1893 when he was suffering a long illness. Miss Lane reproduces the eight pages in facsimile. Eight years later the writer, encouraged by Canon Rawnsley to an interest in her own ability, remembered the letter and borrowed it in order to remodel it as a little book. When the manuscript had been rejected by several publishers, including Warne's, she decided to invest some of her savings in a private edition. Strangeways printed an edition of 250 copies and these were sold to friends, and friends of friends, at one and twopence each.

The private edition is a little book, roughly 5¼″ x 4″, in green boards with a line drawing of the four rabbits on the face. There are 86 unnumbered pages. The first printing is undated, but a later printing ,with minor textual corrections has the date February 1902 on the title-page. Only the frontispiece is in colour. Otherwise the book alternates pages of text and line drawings. The pictures may look drab to those brought up on later coloured illustrations but they are characterised by clean strong line.

This venture had moderate success. The author seems to have made a profit of a pound or two, and was prompted to show a copy of the printed book to Warne's, this time with a satisfactory response. The result was the first commercial edition, which appeared later in 1902. Beatrix Potter redesigned the book completely. Mr Linder has a copy of the private edition in which the author had worked out, in the most professional way, the layout of the new work. Many of the black-and-white illustrations were abandoned, and most of the others were redrawn. All, except the title-page drawing of a very fat, full-faced Peter, were coloured. The drawing gained in mastery, although it might be questioned whether the glamourised Mrs McGregor (later omitted) is better than the grotesque harridan of the first edition (but Beatrix Potter never succeeded in drawing humans except as grotesques). The text was trimmed and made more forceful, notably by the deletion of a long discursive passage, taking up three pages in the private edition, about Mrs Rabbit's domestic economy. Some of this, however, was stored up for use later in *Benjamin Bunny*.

The printing of Warne's edition was in the hands of Edmund Evans. I must confess that the copy I have studied has some very bad registration, much below the standard of that great craftsman. The book was in the now-familiar format, roughly $5\frac{3}{4}''$ x $4\frac{1}{4}''$, with a printed label set in a blind-stamped panel on the cover, and with the characteristic blank backs to the coloured plates. The price was one shilling. It was an immediate success. In a letter (quoted by Miss Quinby) dated October 6, 1902, Beatrix Potter says that the first printing of 6,000 copies was sold out before publication.

Unfortunately the copyright of *Peter Rabbit* was not safeguarded in the United States and the first pirated edition appeared there probably early in the first half of 1903. The subsequent history of the book in the States has been regrettable. Anne Carroll Moore, in *The Art of Beatrix Potter*, describes her first meeting with the book 'in a hideous printed American edition bearing all the stigmata of the new comic strip'. The Cumulative Book List records fourteen American editions between 1930 and 1958 in which the original illustrations were not used, and in some at least of which the story was 'retold'! The dismal list includes one in 'The Cheerie Series', two 'animated' editions, and one retold by Edna Eldredge and Jessie McKee and illustrated by Fern Bisel Peat in 'Old Faithful Books'! Not all the American editions may be as bad as this (a recent one is illustrated by the very distinguished artist Leonard Weisgard), but English readers may permit themselves a Pharisaical feeling of satisfaction that such books may not enter this country.

Peter Rabbit has the charm of most first things, and one need not regret that a book which is often considered a little less than her best should have become the prototype of Beatrix Potter's work, giving its name to the whole series and entering, as few books have done, into the hearts and lives of innumerable people. It has great charm, economy and humour. The backgrounds are less developed than those of later books, and perhaps in consequence have suffered less through the deterioration of the plates in later reprints; but there are some delightful and subtle drawings, the robin finding Peter's shoe among the cabbages, the white cat by the goldfish pond, among others. What must have distinguished it among its contemporaries, apart from excellence of writing and drawing, was its consistency: it depicts throughout, a rabbit-sized world.

Some years earlier, Beatrix Potter had paid a memorable visit to a cousin's at Harescombe Grange in the Cotswolds. Here she heard an entertaining story about a tailor of Gloucester who returned to his shop to find his work all but finished and a note pinned to it complaining: 'No more twist.' The story took shape in her mind, and she later turned it into a manuscript book and sent it to Freda Moore, Noël's sister.

When the success of *Peter Rabbit* set her thinking of material for other books, she turned to the 'mouse book' which had particularly taken her fancy. After all, she had enjoyed the friendship of mice for many years and made many successful drawings of them. A brilliant set of four, to illustrate 'Three little mice sat down to spin', is included in *The Art of Beatrix Potter*, and this, like the picture of the mouse reading *The Day's News*, was ready-made material for the new book. She decided once more to publish privately, and as all sixteen illustrations were in colour the work represented a much greater capital outlay. An edition of 500 copies cost forty pounds.

The private edition of *The Tailor of Gloucester* is dated December 1902. It is a little book, similar in style to *Peter Rabbit*, with a neat line drawing of mice sewing on its pink front board. Some of the atmospheric drawing is particularly fine. For example, the picture of Simkin walking across the snowbound street towards the splash of light in·the tailor's shop, with the rest of the scene bathed in soft moonlight, is masterly.

When later editions were printed, the original drawing had faded (as may be seen in the Tate Gallery), and some of the tonal quality was necessarily lost.

The Warne edition was not published until after *Squirrel Nutkin*, which explains the credit 'Author of ... *The Tale of Squirrel Nutkin*' on the title-page. It appeared in 1903 in the now-familiar form, bearing within a truncated triangle on the cover one of the most charming of all her fancies, the tailor mouse sitting cross-legged on a cotton-reel reading *The Tailor and Cutter*. For this edition three of the original pictures were abandoned, several were redrawn, and seventeen were entirely new.

It might be argued that not all these changes were for the

better. What is certain is that the final book is one of the author's finest, and exhibits if not her most characteristic at least her most accomplished drawing and evocative writing. The story is more compact in plot than most. It has an urban and an 'interior' setting. It is the only book in which a human plays a major part, and even here the tailor, poor man, is sick in bed for almost half the book. The text is longer than any other before *Little Pig Robinson*. Uncharacteristic perhaps, but Beatrix Potter certainly put her best into it. It was her favourite book, and many readers, myself among them, have found in it a richness, a poetical expression, a certain sadness even, which the rest of her work never touches. There are a few signs of artistic immaturity, perhaps. Children have sometimes been troubled because in places the exquisite pictures do not correspond, literally, with the accompanying text. But Beatrix Potter, and the finest of other English artists in this field, never equalled the lovely drawings of fabric and embroidery, of 'crockery and pipkins'. Her many visits to the Victoria and Albert Museum to study costume bore the richest fruit.

In earlier days Bertram had owned an owl. His sister wrote in a letter (reproduced in *The Art of Beatrix Potter*) in 1897, 'The owl hoots all night. If he has a dead mouse he bites its head off then shouts as loud as he can.' In another letter she had touched on the mystery of squirrels who appeared on a Lakeland island when the nuts were ripe—where did they come from? Here was material for a couple of stories, or should it be one? The answer came in a letter to Norah Moore in 1901. The story* follows closely that of *The Tale of Squirrel Nutkin*; indeed almost a third of the text is practically identical in both versions. In later pages there are many divergences, and a comparison of the two provides

* *The Art of Beatrix Potter*, pp. 192-207.

many examples of how a simple tale can be enriched by the addition of telling details. These were added in the published version presumably, to provide an accompanying text for the twenty-seven colour-plates (in the letter there were only twelve little drawings), but the additions are evidence of the author's genius in selection. On the second day of the squirrel's visit to Owl Island, for example, Nutkin tickles old Mr Brown with a nettle and changes his riddle to match. Each day (after the second) the reader sees Nutkin at play while his friends gather nuts. On the fourth day he 'gathered robin's pin-cushions off a briar bush, and stuck them full of pine-needle-pins'. Touches like these give variety and added interest to a repetitive story. The riddles have greater prominence in the printed version, and the answers are embedded in the text. Perhaps Beatrix Potter, or the publisher, thought that not all readers would be as quick at guessing as Norah Moore.

The first edition of *Squirrel Nutkin*, dated 1903, is in the familiar format. The copy I have seen has dark blue boards. On the cover is a roundel with a pasted label of Nutkin skipping. The price was one shilling. A new feature was the decorated end-papers, which for the first time included pictures of the characters in *Peter Rabbit*, *Squirrel Nutkin* and *The Tailor of Gloucester*, joined by flourishes in the now-familiar way.

Although Beatrix Potter seems to have renewed her interest in squirrels during a visit to Long Melford in Suffolk, *Squirrel Nutkin* is a story of the Lake District and the topographical drawing of Derwentwater is the result of much preliminary work. Unfortunately a good deal of the charm of the drawing is lost in recent reprints. Many details, and indeed some of the tone values, are missing, for example the pictures on pages 8, 17 and 41 (8, 15 and 31 in current editions), all of which show the lake and Owl Island. Enough remains to make this one of the most colourful of all the books. The squirrels are consistently delightful, and the artist made the most of the opportunity they offer for design. (The squirrel studies in *The Art of Beatrix Potter* are more a self-conscious exercise in the same: in *Squirrel Nutkin* she is freer and much more skilful.) Another notable feature of *Squirrel Nutkin* is its use of shades of green; some of this gets lost in recent reprints but not all. The grey-green of the fir-cones with which Nutkin played ninepins is firmly contrasted with the greens of dock-leaf and nettle. Throughout the book there is a fine feeling for season; without any of the conventional russet leaves this is clearly autumn.

The Tale of Benjamin Bunny was written as a sequel to *Peter Rabbit* and appears to have been something of a chore. Margaret Lane quotes the author as writing that she was 'glad to get done with rabbits'. The book has little internal evidence of having been done with reluctance. It contains some very fine drawing, and the story has a sharp wry humour.

The first edition is dated 1904. Jane Quinby describes a copy in cloth with an elaborate cover design. The copy I have examined, in light brown boards, is in the conventional format. There have been some slight changes in recent editions, notably in the frontispiece where the original sign above Mrs Rabbit's shop: 'Josephine Rabbit, licensed to sell Tea & Tobacco', has nearly disappeared. Some of the text and one of the illustrations are borrowed from the private edition of *Peter Rabbit*. This text deals with Mrs Rabbit's economy and includes a characteristic personal note ('I once bought a pair [of Mrs Rabbit's muffetees] at a bazaar') which it would have been a pity to lose. And the old buck rabbit smoking rabbit-tobacco, who in *Peter Rabbit* was certainly a digression, is neatly transformed into Old Mr Benjamin Bunny (title page and page 62–78 in the current reprint) who 'had no opinion whatever of cats' and whose switch is not merely for show. The new end-paper design is more elaborate and includes not only Benjamin and the cat but also a hedgehog and a guinea-pig, neither of whom comes into any of the tales, although they appear (as Old Mr Pricklepin and the amiable guinea-pig) thirteen years later in *Appley Dapply's Nursery Rhymes*.

In *The Art of Beatrix Potter* there are six very fine detailed paintings of the garden at Fawe Park, Keswick. These are backgrounds to *Benjamin Bunny* ('I think I have done every imaginable rabbit background'*), and evidence of the infinite care that the artist took. Here you will find the pear tree by which the rabbits entered the garden (but Peter fell head first), the lettuces that Benjamin ate, the little plank-path where the mice 'sat on their doorsteps cracking cherry-stones', two views of the corner by the greenhouse where the rabbits had that unfortunate encounter with the cat, and the garden gate used by Old Mr Bunny.

The drawing of animals and plants is as good and detailed as one would expect. The text too is a model of economy. Benjamin, as hard and practical as his clogs, is neatly characterised in every word and line. With all the fun there is an earnest concern with ordinary things in this book almost more than any other. Mrs Dorothy White says of her daughter's reaction to it (in *Books before Five*), 'Carol found all kinds of unexpected trifles to please her, simple incidents related in some way to her own daily life at home'.

Beatrix Potter had brought home from her visit to Gloucestershire not only the idea for a wonderful book but

* *Tale of Beatrix Potter*, p. 77.

two mice rescued from a trap. They were Tom Thumb and Hunca Munca. The latter became a great favourite, a lady mouse of character. She was destined to have her share of immortality as the heroine of *The Tale of Two Bad Mice*.

Margaret Lane tells the tragi-comic story of how this story was written, with the co-operation of Norman Warne and the opposition of the Potters. Nothing of these difficulties shows in the charming book which was published in 1904, and was dedicated to Winifred Warne, 'the little girl who had the doll's house'.

Two Bad Mice is a book written and drawn to scale (see, for example, the fly on the doll's house roof on page 44–32 in recent reprints). No human intrudes in this miniature world bounded by doll's house and mouse hole. The dumbness of the dolls—Lucinda showed a little emotion at seeing the havoc wrought in her house by the mice, but Jane only smiled—contrasts delightfully with the animation of the two mice. These are real animals, undoubtedly drawn from life. Of all the Peter Rabbit books this is perhaps the most immediately accessible to small children. Everything is within their experience but everything seen so clearly and with such a skill in interpretation that the book both confirms and extends the reader's experience. Carol White[*] said, after hearing the story for the first time, 'I love it, I love it. Again!' and that has been the immediate reaction of generations of children.

It is to be regretted that so much of the detail, particularly of wallpaper and other designs in Winifred Warne's little house, is lost in modern reprints.

Margaret Lane tells of an early pet, a hedgehog named (of course) Tiggy, who succumbed quickly to a too civilised

[*] *Books before Five*, by Dorothy White. New Zealand Council for Educational Research, 1954, p. 105.

diet. Mrs Tiggy-Winkle was tougher and survived many years of affection-filled captivity, including holiday travel with her mistress. On one of these journeys Mrs Tiggy-Winkle was introduced to a little girl on a Cumberland farm called Lucie. Out of this meeting came *The Tale of Mrs Tiggy-Winkle*, a story which, for all its obvious faults, has always won the very personal love of readers.

The background drawings, so important in this book, were done in the Lake country and the drawings of the animal heroine, with the help both of Mrs Tiggy-Winkle and of a stuffed model, in London. The book appeared in 1905, in an edition distinguished mainly by a very full advertisement on the back of the dust-jacket for the Peter Rabbit books and on the front flap an advance blurb for *The Pie and the Patty-Pan*.

There are two principal weaknesses in *The Tale of Mrs Tiggy-Winkle*. The plot is very thin, almost non-existent, and the concluding transformation of the homely 'very stout short person' into 'nothing but a Hedgehog' is clumsily contrived and difficult for small children to accept. An equally important disadvantage is the figure of Lucie. In *The Art of Beatrix Potter* there is a page of trial sketches of Lucie; a back view, several faces, feet and legs. They are evidence, if any were needed, that humans were beyond Beatrix Potter's range, and Lucie, who appears in sixteen of the twenty-seven plates, is just not well enough drawn. Everything else in the book is masterly. The mountain setting is most beautifully conveyed—even poor modern reprints have not lost all the magic of the view above Little-town (page 17—15 in the current reprint)—and Mrs Tiggy-Winkle's kitchen illustrates the artist's skill in creating atmosphere by a multitude of tiny details. As for the heroine, she is one of the nicest and most complete of all the animal characters; very definitely a craftswoman—not a laundress but 'an excellent clear-starcher'—and a kindly person taking pride in her work and an interest, critical but helpful, in her customers. A feature of the book, and one that children enjoy, is the link with the previous books. When Mrs Tiggy-Winkle complains that Mrs Rabbit's red handker-chief smells of onions, every reader of *Benjamin Bunny* knows why; and at the mention of Nutkin's 'red tail-coat with no tail' and 'a much-shrunk blue jacket belonging to Peter Rabbit' the listening children exchange knowing glances.

VI. The Works—Tales of Sawrey

Benjamin Bunny had been dedicated 'to the children of Sawrey', but *The Pie and the Patty-Pan* was the first book to be set in the village which was to be Beatrix Potter's home and the scene of many of her books. It appeared in 1905 in a larger format (approximately $7\frac{1}{4}'' \times 5\frac{1}{2}''$) and with elaborately decorated covers. The copy I have seen has an ornate ribbon design with a roundel enclosing a cat who is almost too pretty to be bearable. The book has several unusual features. The text is long. Only ten of the illustrations are in colour, the rest being line drawing. The colour-plates are provided with captions, and they are, for technical reasons, not always placed correctly in the text.

The Pie and the Patty-Pan has some delightful drawing, particularly in colour, and is of considerable topographical interest. As a story for children it is a little less than perfect. The plot is excessively complex, and children, understandably, have difficulty in following its course. There is considerable charm in the social conversations but these are too long for very small readers. The blemishes are many; they are perhaps a small price to pay for many homely interior scenes and enchanting glimpses of the village and its surroundings.

The red boards of *Mr Jeremy Fisher* in 1906 enclosed what is one of the author's greatest *tours de force*. Once again, and perhaps more successfully than in any other book, she shows the scale of the world of small creatures. Mr Jeremy Fisher inhabits his own world, with his own delightfully waterlogged house, his boat, his friends, his appetite. Everything is in scale. Then comes disaster. He is swallowed by a trout. The great creature, head to tail filling the picture diagonally, immediately brings home the smallness of Jeremy's world. All ends well, and the reader sees him, recovered and clothed again, entertaining his distinguished friends in the most urbane fashion. The memory remains however; Mr Jeremy Fisher is a very small great man.

The book—which like so many others originated in a picture-letter—has always been a particular favourite with children, for it contains so much that is dear to them. Mr Fisher's house, for example, is a child's dream house, the house where no one scolds. 'Mr Jeremy liked getting his feet wet; nobody ever scolded him, and he never caught a cold!' His fishing expedition is a child's joy, too, for all that it rained and the day nearly ended in tragedy. His boat, his tackle, everything is as a child would see it.

The drawing is very fine. Although the predominating tone is pale green there is no monotony, and the glimpses of rain-washed Lakeland—sadly faded though they are in present day reprints—are full of enchantment. Beatrix Potter had a sound instinct when and how to clothe her characters, and she is singularly happy here. Mr Fisher himself is Pickwickian (as Miss Lane points out). How like frogs' legs his tight pantaloons are! He has a natural elegance which makes even sharper the loss of his galoshes (which the trout ate) and the damage to that macintosh which he was providentially wearing. His friends too, are masterly. Sir Isaac Newton, in tail coat, dress trousers (a little too long) and showy black and gold waistcoat, is the aristocrat gone to seed. Mr Alderman Ptolemy Tortoise has the imposing presence of the man of affairs. It comes as a shock to realise that, chain of office apart, he is naked!

Beatrix Potter felt for this book the affection of the

creator for something quite original. After all those rabbits and mice, it had been a pleasant change to enter another world and to seek out the latent beauty and humour in very different creatures. Mr Jeremy Fisher and his friends feature prominently in the miniature letters which she wrote for child friends and put into a tiny G.P.O. sack like the one now in Mr Linder's possession. (It is illustrated in *The Art of Beatrix Potter*.)

Miss Moppet and *A Fierce Bad Rabbit* stand a little aside from the body of Beatrix Potter's work. They are 'stories', not 'tales'; though in fact neither has much of a story. They were both issued originally in wallet form and only very recently have they been accorded the format of the other books. They are brief (15 pictures including a cover plate, compared with 27 in the normal volume). One might say they are light weight; but *Miss Moppet* at least has her share of admirers. From Boys and Girls Book House in Toronto comes the story of a three-year-old boy who came under her spell while his father was away in the services. On the day of his father's discharge, Mother came to the library for *Miss Moppet*. She explained, 'He feels it would be a terrible thing if his father were to go through the rest of his life without knowing Miss Moppet.' A girl reading *Miss Moppet* in the same library told the librarian, 'This is the book I like best. I always take it out. I bring it back and go and look for another copy to take home again.' Not many books will inspire such devotion.

Neither book is dated on its title page, although each bears on its flap 'copyright—1906 . . .' The original format was unusual. Each 'book' was a neat cloth wallet, *Miss Moppet* grey, *A Fierce Bad Rabbit* green, with a tuck-in flap. When opened, the 'book' appears as a long strip of alternate text and pictures, folded concertinawise, and reinforced by a linen backing. Such a format has the charm of novelty, but makes for neither economy nor durability. It was hardly surprising therefore that later editions reverted to a conventional book form. The original wallets were very small ($4\frac{1}{4}'' \times 3\frac{3}{4}''$ roughly); in book-form they were enlarged to roughly $5'' \times 4\frac{1}{4}''$, which is still appreciably less than the 'Peter Rabbit' books. In book form the two stories are undated, but appear to have been issued about 1913.

Miss Moppet was one of the kittens of Mrs Tabitha Twitchit—Beatrix Potter had a sure instinct for the memorable and exactly right name—and she appeared again with her brother and sister in *The Tale of Tom Kitten* which was published in 1907.

Beatrix had bought Hill Top in 1905 and in a sense *Tom Kitten* was the fine first fruit of this venture, for Hill Top, and particularly its garden, is the scene of this most approachable story. Some of her plots have been criticised as complicated. Here is one that is crystal-clear and based moreover on a situation painfully familiar to most children. Mrs Tabitha Twitchit (who 'owned' Hill Top, cat-fashion, in reality) has invited fine company to tea, and washes and dresses her children so that they may do her credit. When they were ready she 'unwisely turned them out into the garden, to be out of the way . . .' How many mothers have regretted just such unwisdom? (Mrs Nesbit did, on the occasion when her sons 'planted' Daisy—who was to become E. Nesbit—because in her party-frock she looked as pretty as a flower.) It is inevitable that the kittens will spoil their clothes; where Beatrix Potter surprises us is by bringing in the Puddle-Ducks who dress themselves in the kittens' clothes. The denouement has the relentless inevitability of Greek tragedy!

There is fine observation not only in the lovely pictures

but also in the writing. On the rare occasions that Beatrix uses description, it is sharply pointed. The ducks 'had very small eyes and looked surprised'. *Tom Kitten* is an example of how the animals put on character with their clothes. Look at Mr Drake Puddle-Duck (page 56—70 in the current reprint), anonymously ducklike, advancing on the clothes. In the next picture, having put them on (they fitted terribly), he has suddenly acquired individuality and an urbane manner. ' "It's a very fine morning!" said Mr Drake Puddle-Duck.' Tom, too, during his toilet is pure kitten. Dressed Kate Greenaway fashion he is Kitten-plus.

The garden scenes give enduring delight in this book. There are countless details for the small child to find for himself, of flower and tree and butterfly. It is a pity that so many fine effects—particularly in the landscape painting on pages 35 and 47—are blurred when they appear (on pages 27 and 35) in modern reprints. The colour in the first edition is exquisite.

The next book, *The Tale of Jemima Puddle-Duck*, appeared in 1908. Jemima Puddle-Duck was a real inhabitant of the Hill Top farmyard, and her Red-Riding-Hood-like adventure has the ring of truth. The story indeed starts in a completely naturalistic way with a farmyard scene including one of Beatrix Potter's unsuccessful attempts at drawing humans. Artistically many of the drawings are not completely satisfactory. Am I alone, I wonder, in finding the collie Kep (of whom the artist made a larger study in the following year—page 134 in *The Art of Beatrix Potter*) inadequate? He, and the other farm dogs, stand aside from the other characters (in this and other books) in having no added human characteristics. They remain all dog. It is significant that, except for John Joiner and Pickles, none of Beatrix

Potter's dogs wear clothes. They are workers on the farm and are to be taken seriously.

This is essentially an open-air story. The landscape drawing is of her best, particularly the scenes when Jemima sets off over the hill in search of a safe place, free of 'superfluous' hens, for her nest. In the second of these there is an enchanting glimpse of Esthwaite Water below. There are delicate clouds in the picture (page 23—19 in current reprints) where Jemima tries to fly, but these like many other fine details, have all but vanished in recent editions. From her earliest years Beatrix had been an exact painter of flowers, and the foxgloves among which the gentleman in sandy whiskers appropriately has his home are among her finest of this kind.

If *Tom Kitten* and *Jemima Puddle-Duck* represent the outdoor life of Sawrey, *The Roly-Poly Pudding* shows the interior of Hill Top most successfully. *The Roly-Poly Pudding* appeared first in 1908 in a most elaborate and attractive edition, price 2s. 6d. It was the largest book to date (approximately 8" × 6¾"), in red cloth lettered in green. The title-page has an elaborate ornamented design, headed by Samuel Whiskers seated on his rolling-pin, with kittens and rats and, centred at the foot, Tom Kitten in his coat of pudding. Under the credit 'Author of *The Tale of Peter Rabbit*' come four little rabbits in outline. The design is pulled together by formal flourishes. All this is reproduced in modern editions but with the reduction in size of page much of the charm of the design is gone. A pleasant feature of the original edition, not used now, was a mock bookplate on the half-title page with Samuel Whiskers' coat-of-arms and the inscription 'Samuel Whiskers His Book'. The dedication was to the real Sammy, 'an affectionate little friend and most accomplished thief'. Instead of the familiar end-papers showing characters in the stories, this book had (and still retains) designs, different front and back, showing the depredations of Samuel Whiskers and his family among bags of meal, oats, potatoes and bran. When the book was redesigned to match the 'Peter Rabbit' books (in 1926), the title was changed to *The Tale of Samuel Whiskers; or, The Roly-Poly Pudding*, although the original title was retained in the American edition.

Like *The Pie and the Patty-Pan* it has a long text and is illustrated in line as well as in colour. The story is a complicated and slightly macabre one, but has nevertheless been a particular favourite with children. The theme is familiar to them—who has not taken evasive action when mother wants the children in a safe place?—and the climb up the chimney and the journey through the mouse-passages are a common fantasy. It is the house that gives unity to a story which becomes a little untidy in the telling. Children who enjoy the story know the house intimately; the elegant staircase, the kitchen range by which Tom made his rash ascent and where Mrs Twitchit told the visitor her sad story, the roof with its sturdy towerlike chimney and enchanting view over the orchards, the nooks and crannies of Samuel Whiskers' domain. There is some very fine characteristic drawing in this book. Samuel Whiskers himself, fat and indolent as any Eastern potentate, sitting with hands across his vast belly, his scrawny spouse Anna Maria—how is it that they can be at once so rat-like, so sinister (in a human sense) and so likable? One's relief that Mrs Tabitha Twitchit is rid of them at the end of the story is tempered with satisfaction that they made a safe escape to poor Farmer Potatoes' barn. And surely this artist never painted a more pleasing picture than that of Mrs Ribby, dressed for visiting in bonnet and shawl, apron and lavender dress, with the

Spring garden behind her. Beatrix Potter herself appears in the text: John Joiner 'regretted that he had not time to stay to dinner, because he had just finished making a wheelbarrow for Miss Potter, and she had ordered two hen-coops'; and in the picture of Samuel Whiskers' flight her shadowy figure is just seen at the end of the lane.

In the next book the scene moves from Sawrey. *The Tale of the Flopsy Bunnies* (1909) was written in response to a demand for more about Peter Rabbit and was dedicated 'For all little friends of Mr McGregor & Peter & Benjamin'. It had the common weakness of enforced sequels; only the most partisan admirers would say it is among Beatrix Potter's best work. The story has some nice touches of humour, and occasionally there is felicity in drawing—the youngest Flopsy Bunny at the window listening to Mr McGregor, for example—but in general the drawing is less good and there is less enjoyment of fine details.

Mr McGregor's garden in *Benjamin Bunny* had been in Cumberland, but Beatrix, on holiday in Wales, drew the pictures for *The Flopsy Bunnies* at the lovely house of Gwaynynog, a little outside Denbigh. In *The Art of Beatrix Potter* there are two pictures of the house, a good painting of one corner of a room with clock and dresser, and a better sepia drawing, wonderful in perspective and detail, of the same dresser, three-tiered against the panelled wall. Unfortunately *The Flopsy Bunnies* is an open-air story, and at Gwaynynog Beatrix seems to have found none of the delight of Fawe Park.

One of the better pictures in the first edition was, inexplicably, redrawn for later editions. The original appears in *The Art of Beatrix Potter*. Mr and Mrs Benjamin Bunny, with their family, are passing Peter Rabbit's nursery garden. On the wall is a notice: 'Peter Rabbit & Mother—Florists—

Gardens neatly razed. Borders devastated by the Night or Year.' Later, this delightful board was omitted and instead there is a glimpse, amid lettuces, of Peter in his blue jacket. Was it the objections to 'soporific', 'improvident', and other splendid words that decided the author to remove so nobly worded a notice-board?

In 1909 too appeared *Ginger and Pickles*. This was another large book (a little smaller than *The Pie and the Patty-Pan*) and like the other books in larger format it had both line and colour illustrations. The end-paper designs marked a quite new departure. On the front end-papers in two pictures without words is the drama of the rescue of a mouse trapped in a jar. At the back Ginger and Pickles' scales are being used, first to prove that two mice equal two other mice (or is the fifth mouse surreptitiously tipping the scale?), secondly to show how much more Alderman Ptolemy Tortoise weighs than Jeremy Fisher (Sir Isaac Newton assists). These amusing designs are retained in current editions.

Ginger and Pickles is a book of Sawrey; it contains more-over a roll-call of previous characters. Among the customers at Ginger and Pickles' shop are Peter Rabbit and Benjamin Bunny, Lucinda and Jane (of the Warne dolls' house), Samuel Whiskers and Anna Maria, Jeremy Fisher, Mrs Tiggy-Winkle, Squirrel Nutkin (who seems to be stealing from a sack of nuts left, unwisely, outside), Jemima Puddle-Duck, and sundry unnamed mice. Tom Kitten, Moppet and Mittens peer through the window, and their mother Mrs Tabitha Twitchit keeps the rival establishment in the village ('She did not give credit').

The real shop in Sawrey was kept by bedridden old Mr John Taylor, to whom the book is dedicated, and who is included in the story as Mr John Dormouse who 'stayed in bed, and would say nothing but "very sorry"; which is no way of carrying on a retail business'. Was it for his sake that the story was dragged out after the departure of Ginger and Pickles, to the detriment of the artistic unity? The truth is, I fancy, that Beatrix Potter was so much in love with her village that she found it difficult to end this story of her neighbours.

Apart from the untidy ending the story is a difficult one for children, who find the economics of shopkeeping as difficult as did Ginger and Pickles. Even with the author's explanations 'credit' is a difficult concept for small children, and what do they make of bills sent 'with compts'? The book is good fun and excellent in illustration, but with many readers it must be accounted a failure.

A little girl in Toronto says, 'I want [the book] about the clean mouse that asked the frog to dinner'. Mr Jackson wasn't really *asked* to dinner, but Mrs Tittlemouse was certainly clean. Thomasina Tittlemouse saved the Flopsy Bunnies from a dreadful fate and was rewarded with enough rabbit-wool to make 'a cloak and a hood, and a handsome muff and a pair of warm mittens'. Such a charming creature deserved a book of her own and it came in 1910.

The Tale of Mrs Tittlemouse is the story I remember most clearly from childhood, and I have always loved it dearly. It lacks the subtlety of the best of Beatrix Potter, and there are many with more exquisite pictures, but it has the virtue of simplicity and a positive quality of writing which makes it particularly memorable. Mrs Tittlemouse is the type of all distracted housewives who cannot make others live up to their standards, but she is a character as well as a type. The setting gives little opportunity for colourful and detailed drawing, and it is interesting to see how the artist varies her pictures within the same underground scene. The drawing of the various intruders, beetles, bees, ladybirds, butterflies, spiders, is precise and dramatic. As for Mr Jackson (toad, not frog) he is one of Beatrix Potter's happiest inventions. 'Tiddly, widdly, widdly, Mrs Tittlemouse!' haunted my childhood. They were perhaps the first truly poetic words I ever knew.

It may be that the grey squirrel has much less charm than his red cousin, but *The Tale of Timmy Tiptoes* (1911) is something of a failure. There are some good things in it, such as the scene (page 26—20 in current reprints) in which the squirrels are digging up nuts in a glade backed by forest and mountain, and the character of Chippy Hackee, that disreputable wife-biter and good companion. Possibly the alien setting did not suit the artist; chipmunks are not to be found in the Lakes and certainly not bears! The landscape scenes are less carefully drawn, and there is little personality in the minor animal characters; Silvertail, the only character apart from principals to have a name, is hardly to be distinguished from his fellows. The text too, has little of the memorable quality of earlier books.

The Tale of Mr Tod (1912) shows some deterioration in detail of the illustrations but the story is of the first quality. The book is longer than most and, like *The Pie and the Patty-Pan* and *The Roly-Poly Pudding*, is illustrated with many drawings in line as well as fifteen (sixteen including the elaborate cover-label) in colour. *Mr Tod* is a suspense story worked out in considerable detail and written with a conscious craftsmanship rare in Beatrix Potter. There is nothing elsewhere in her work comparable to the building up of tension as the two rabbits follow the trail of the kidnapping Tommy Brock, and the description of night falling outside the house is of almost nightmare quality. The fight at the climax of the story is splendidly done, subtly too, as it is seen entirely from the viewpoint of the rabbits who are reluctant witnesses of the epic struggle.

The length of the story, and its complexity, make it a book for children rather older than those who have enjoyed the simple excitement of *Peter Rabbit*. This presumably is the reason for the dedication, 'For Francis William of Ulva—someday!' Miss Lane quotes a letter from this Francis, a nephew, referring to *Johnny Town-Mouse*, published six years later. From the spelling he was still over-young for the sophisticated charm of Tommy Brock.

Much of the drawing in *Mr Tod* is not very good. There is little quality in the line drawings, and in the coloured plates one often looks in vain for the exquisite detail which makes each picture in the earlier books an adventure in discovery. There is some decline in the graphic delineation of character. Mr Tod and Mr Brock are portrayed admirably in words; the former lacks, in the drawings, that urbanity which gave style to the 'sandy-whiskered gentleman' in *Jemima Puddle-Duck*. The author maligns the badger—in nature it is Tommy Brock who suffers from Mr Tod's lack of personal hygiene—and she fails to capture his homely charms. This may be deliberate; he is the villain of this piece. Perhaps the nicest touch in the story is the portrait of old Mr Bouncer, Benjamin Bunny's father, now 'stricken in years' and no longer a terror to cats and delinquent young relatives. The poor old rabbit, living in fear of his daughter-in-law's discipline—she takes away his pipe and rabbit-tobacco—and her retributive spring-cleaning, is almost painfully real.

For the first edition of *Mr Tod* Beatrix Potter designed a new and most elaborate end-paper. This showed Mr Samuel Whiskers, as bill-sticker, setting up a giant poster of the 'Peter Rabbit' books with the cover-label of *Mr Tod* boldly featured. Looking on are most of the characters in the books, dressed in their best, and the whole is given a charming landscape setting. (A modified version of the design is now used for the two 'stories' and the nursery-rhyme books.)

In the last book before her marriage, the last perhaps in which her full powers are shown, the author herself appears. Although, by a delightful transference, the owner of Pigling Bland's farm is Aunt Pettitoes, worthiest of all sows, Beatrix Potter plays a considerable role in the earlier part of the story, and is drawn, featureless, on pages 22 and 24. It seems to me that *The Tale of Pigling Bland* was written with great affection and it inspires affection in its readers. I have always loved it beyond its intrinsic merits, and it is a favourite with innumerable children. Miss Jean Thomson tells of a boy in Toronto, meeting Pigling for the first time exclaiming, 'I didn't know a pig could shake hands with a rooster but here he is doing it!'

In *The Tale of Pigling Bland* Beatrix was successful in one of the most difficult tasks which come a writer's way. She made an entirely good person interesting. Pigling's brothers and sisters (except Spot) are in one degree or another wicked or mischievous; Pigling is unfailing in courtesy and understanding. In him all piggy virtues are gathered. Responsible, brave, resourceful, it is good to think that at the end of the story he is on the way to fulfilling his ambition to 'have a little garden and grow potatoes'. Aunt Pettitoes is a memorable character, too. In her address to her departing sons she rises to lyrical and dramatic heights untouched in the Beatrix Potter stories since *The Tailor of Gloucester*.

' "Now Pigling Bland, son Pigling Bland, you must go to market. Take your brother Alexander by the hand. Mind your Sunday clothes, and remember to blow your nose . . .

beware of traps, hen roosts, bacon and eggs; always walk upon your hind legs".'

This is a literary tale. The drawing is uneven in quality. At its best, in the picture of Aunt Pettitoes with her greedy litter, in the cover drawing of Pigling at the cross-roads, possibly in the drawing of Pigling eating his porridge by the fire, it is full of fun and character. It seldom has the feeling for landscape of the artist's best work. The writing is nearly as good as her best elsewhere, and the plot is handled with a nice feeling for its dramatic quality. 1913 marks the end of an important stage in Beatrix Potter's life. In *Pigling Bland* she says a tender, humorous farewell to her old life.

VII. The Works—by Mrs Heelis

Mrs Heelis was a busy woman who only rarely had time, and the desire, to yield to the entreaties of her admirers for another book. Miss Lane quotes one letter saying tartly, 'When *I* was a little girl, *I* was satisfied with about six books . . . I think that children now have too many.' The books produced during the years of her married life are for the most part based on earlier ideas or sketches. They are never without characteristic touches of humour or sharp observation; rarely do they enrich the reader with a new experience as almost all her earlier work had done.

Appley Dapply's Nursery Rhymes—a tiny book $5'' \times 4\frac{1}{4}''$— came out in 1917. The first edition is undated. The companion volume, *Cecily Parsley's Nursery Rhymes*, appeared, again without a date, in 1922. They may conveniently be considered together. It seems clear that much, if not all, of the material of these little books belongs to a much earlier date. Appley Dapply comes into a picture-letter written to Hilda Moore in 1904, which is reproduced in Miss Quinby's Check List. She was a brown mouse 'who bit off Pippin's tail'. Elsewhere she appears as a companion of Hunca Munca, the heroine of *Two Bad Mice*. The frontispiece to *Appley Dapply*, an unrelated picture of two prosperous gentlemen-rabbits walking in the snow, is similar in style to Beatrix Potter's earliest published drawings of about 1893. Old Mr Pricklepin (page 29) made his (or should it be 'her', for the model was surely Mrs Tiggy-Winkle) first appearance in the end-papers of *Benjamin Bunny* (1904); and this also was the source of the 'amiable guinea-pig' who is the subject of the last rhyme. From *Cecily Parsley*, the first draft of 'Ninny Ninny Netticoat' is reproduced in *The Art of Beatrix Potter* with the date 1897, and an alternative version of the guinea-pig's garden is reproduced in the same book. The scene of 'Bow, wow, wow!' is the product of an earlier holiday in the South, Sussex from the architectural evidence.

If the two books of nursery rhymes are a heterogeneous collection they contain some of the artist's best drawing, particularly in *Cecily Parsley*. The two interiors of the Pen Inn have a homely charm, and Mistress Pussy's kitchen is as beautifully observed in its harmonious detail as the best pictures of Hill Top in *The Roly-Poly Pudding*. There are some delightful touches of original humour. Who else would have thought that 'my lady' into whose chamber goosey goosey gander intruded was a sow?

Early attempts to translate Aesop into homely English terms are recorded in *The Art of Beatrix Potter*. *Johnny Town-Mouse* (published, undated, in 1918), whatever its actual date of composition, belongs in manner to an early period. The concern with detail, of materials or flowers, is as absorbed, and the invention of character is as strong. The Beatrix Potter of *Tom Kitten* days would, however, have made more of the mouse-eye view of the town house. The staircase (page 41—31 in current reprints) has received perfunctory treatment, and the dresser (page 35—27 in current reprints) is unworthy of the hand which had drawn the Welsh dresser at Gwaynynog.

One fault of the book, from a child's point of view, is the failure of the pictures to match exactly with the story. Children find it difficult to understand why Timmy Willie, while staying with Johnny Town-Mouse, is shown in two consecutive pictures enjoying life in the country.

Timmy Willie is an important addition to Beatrix Potter's gallery of portraits. He is a fully realised character, interesting in his own right and an excellent foil to the sharp-witted and sharp-worded Johnny. His final portrait, with sunshade and strawberry luncheon, is delightful.

In 1927 an American publisher, Alexander McKay, visited Sawrey to attempt to coax a new book out of the busy Mrs Heelis. She had no time, perhaps no inclination, perhaps no invention, for new work, but among many notes for work never completed there might be material for a book, something quite different and for American friends only. There was, and in 1929 the David McKay Company published *The Fairy Caravan*. The author published a very small English edition 'by Beatrix Heelis' in order to safeguard copyright, but a commercial edition did not appear in this country until 1952. Its history has therefore been very different in the two countries. Bertha Mahoney Miller* writes of her granddaughter stroking the book and saying, 'Oh, lovely *Fairy Caravan*, if only there were ten of you!' In England there has been no *Fairy Caravan* tradition. Part of the pleasure of *Peter Rabbit* is that it is a pleasure shared with mother—and grandmother. There is as yet no second generation of *Fairy Caravan* readers here. Moreover, in 1952 the book appeared in competition with much competent mediocrity; fifty years earlier the star of *Peter Rabbit* blazed in almost solitary splendour.

How good is *The Fairy Caravan*? It is enormously interesting to adult admirers for the light it sheds on the writer, her background, and her idea of what was worth writing. There are in it bits and pieces of several possibly good books in her usual manner. The book is as a whole untidy, ill-proportioned, often dull. The drawings are

* *Horn Book*, May 1941.

nearly all poor. She had told Warne's of failing sight in 1928 when she had done the delicate colour-work for *Peter Rabbit's Almanac*. This is sadly evident in *The Fairy Caravan*, where she is unable to do justice to her own invention in the characters of Tuppenny, Xarifa and Paddy Pig. Paddy is in essence one of her best ideas, and his sufferings at the hands of the nurse-manquée Mary Ellen, a 'fat tabby cat with . . . an unnecessary purry manner' are richly comic. Tuppenny, the guinea-pig whose hair responded only too well to Messrs Ratton and Scratch's elixir, and who made his first appearance very early in the Beatrix Potter story*, might in other circumstances have been the hero of an excellent picture-story. After the first chapter he loses his way in *The Fairy Caravan*.

Writing in *Horn Book* (May 1942) Beatrix Potter had described how she found the prints of fairy horses on Troutbeck Fell and how 'the finding of those little fairy footmarks on the old drove road first made me aware of the Fairy Caravan'. Undoubtedly the book meant much to her—there was much of herself and her Lakeland life in it—and for that reason it must mean much to those who love her work and who treasure every hint of her personality, much as she treasured every feather from her beloved Charles the rooster's tail. It is nevertheless a sad book, as every work of fading genius must be sad.

The last book written and illustrated by Beatrix Potter was *The Tale of Little Pig Robinson*, published in 1930 at 3s. 6d. An American edition was published in the same year by McKay of Philadelphia. *Little Pig Robinson* appeared in the large format, like the original edition of *The Roly-Poly Pudding*. A distinctive feature of the first edition was the design for the end-papers (no longer used). On the front

*The Art of Beatrix Potter, pp. 186–8 in the second edition.

end-paper appeared Susan the cat, looking down at 'The Pound of Candles', and on the right the ship sailing away; at the back was a view of the tug *Sea Horse*, and the owl and the pussy-cat approaching their honeymoon island.

Despite its present format, this book does not belong to the Peter Rabbit tradition, and perhaps for that reason it has been less enjoyed than some of the others. Miss Lane calls it 'very dull'. This is unkind. There is much good in the book, if none of the author's best. The story is developed from a picture-letter (reproduced in *The Art of Beatrix Potter*) dated 1894. It is a long story, it must be admitted, far too long, and not well planned. A disproportionate amount of space is given to Robinson's walk to market. No doubt this is the part which the author liked best, but the story demands better construction than this. For the first and only time too, Beatrix Potter took one eye off nature and wrote the fanciful stuff which adults imagine that children like. When Robinson reaches his island he finds trees growing acid drops and sweets, and bread trees which grow 'iced cakes and muffins, ready baked'. The false note jars immediately.

Altogether, for all its length, this is a light-weight story. At its best it is something which the author had already done better. Robinson is no Pigling Bland, and his aunts, although their farewell speech is an echo of Aunt Pettitoes' lack the personality of their great prototype. The walk to market, however, is described with real feeling, and the story conveys something of the confused bustle of a country market. On the whole the illustrations are poor, the country scenes lacking in telling detail, and Mrs Flock, the keeper of the wool-shop, a shadow of Tenniel's drawing. One coloured picture alone reminds one of the halcyon days: Robinson in the High Street, a nice muddle of humans and animals among the shop-fronts behind him, and in the foreground a brilliant study of a cock and hen driving a trap. This has in it a rare touch of satirical comedy.

There remain three minor works, not published in un-limited editions in this country, and without the author's illustrations. The first, and the strangest of these is *Sister Anne* which was published in America in 1932. This is a long novel based on the tale of Bluebeard. There is very little of Beatrix Potter in this book, other than the Lanca-shire setting and one or two glimpses of country life. One can see a little of the life of Hill Top in the description of Fatima whose 'rake set the pace in the hayfield', but the extra-ordinary 'period' language which the principal characters use is a sad decline from the elegant mannered conversation of Mrs Tabitha Twitchit and Mrs Ribby.

Beatrix Potter's last gift to her American friends was a little story written in 1943 and first published in *Horn Book* in May 1944. This was *Wag-by-Wall*, a sentimental tale about an old countrywoman whose fortunes are retrieved at the last possible moment by the fall of an owlet down her chimney which reveals a stocking full of gold. There is not much intrinsic merit in the story, except perhaps in the observation, sharp as ever, of the behaviour of the cow and the owls.

The last published work of Beatrix Potter is *The Tale of the Faithful Dove*, a story written in 1907 and published by Warne's in America in 1956 with pleasant illustrations by an unnamed artist. It tells the story of Mr Tiddler, a Rye pigeon whose wife Amabella, avoiding the attack of a hawk, takes refuge in the chimney of a deserted house. Here she is befriended by a mouse and eventually rescued with her new-born son Tobias.

The story has some charm, particularly in the conversation between the trapped pigeon and her benefactors, a mouse of great gentility whose manners and costume are out of *The Tailor of Gloucester*. One is aware all the time, however, of the lack of the author's illustrations. With them the text could have been reduced by more than half and the story sharpened.

VII. The Beatrix Potter Industry

Out of the enormous devotion that these little books inspired sprang the Beatrix Potter industry. Margaret Lane tells amusingly of the naïve lady who made a nursery frieze out of Peter Rabbit and asked Beatrix Potter if she thought the publishers would mind if she had it printed! The ingenuous Mrs Garnett was not the first to see potential profit in this material. Beatrix Potter had before this been incensed by the sight of toy models of her characters, of German origin, which under the shelter of Free Trade had flooded the English market. (' "Bite him!" spluttered Ginger [seeing the policeman] "he's only a German doll!" '). Her anger drove her to the only political activity of her life. Tighter copyright restrictions made it possible for Warne's to keep control over the standard of reproduction of Beatrix Potter figures in a wide variety of forms. Sandersons found her frieze design 'old-fashioned' fifty years ago but present-day versions continue to sell and presumably will continue to do so for ever and ever. The current Warne list includes in addition pictures mounted for hanging (in these the drawings are enlarged to an uncomfortable degree), jig-saw puzzles and a Peter Rabbit race-game. There are also on the market mugs, plates and other nursery crockery, and a series of china figures (produced since 1948 by John Beswick Ltd of Longton) which are perhaps the most satisfactory of all interpretations of the characters in three dimensions. In the book version of *The Story of Miss Moppet* (*c.* 1913) there is an advertisement for 'Peter Rabbit's slippers. The "Joy" footwear for tiny feet. 3s. 6d. per pair'. These do not appear to be still on the market!

Today, when the commercial exploitation of film and television 'characters' is a commonplace, the Beatrix Potter industry excites no comment. What is noteworthy, however, is that the industry had a literary origin, and that it has kept faithfully to the original drawings. No other characters from books have become so completely a part of the nursery tradition, except possibly Gollywog, and he persists in spite, not because of his literary origin. The bits and pieces of the Beatrix Potter industry have all served to send children back to the books.

Dramatic adaptations of the stories had a limited success. Harcourt Williams made two little one-act plays for the Christmas Matinées which his wife, Jean Sterling Mackinlay, presented every year. *The Tailor of Gloucester*, with its compact plot and unity of action, would seem made for dramatic treatment, and on the stage the play must have had some charm. Unfortunately there is little dialogue in the original: the tailor's distracted monologue does not make for drama and Simpkin says little but 'Miaw' and 'Dilly, dilly, dilly'. Harcourt Williams used Beatrix Potter's words when he could, and these stick out from the flatness of the invented dialogue. He changed the story comparatively little except to make too much of Simpkin's repentance, and why ever did he make that most uncompromising of toms 'Dame' Simpkin? He was more successful with *Ginger and Pickles*, possibly because the original is less perfect. The story tails off untidily and the dramatist was probably wise to give his play a neat happy ending, thereby softening Beatrix Potter's ruthlessness. He turned to dramatic account a great many hints in the story, with the result that the play has movement and is never entirely false to the story, although, like

The Tailor of Gloucester, it lacks the incomparable atmosphere of the original. The dramatised *Mr Samuel Whiskers*
by Theron H. Butterworth is a neat, but undistinguished,
little play. It is probably the best for young amateur players,
and it copes adequately with the technical problems of
staging a complicated story. Inevitably the invented dialogue
sits uneasily beside the words borrowed from the original.

Christopher le Fleming published in 1935 his two books
of Peter Rabbit music. (*The Peter Rabbit Music Books for
Pianoforte.* Chester—later called *Beatrix Potter Suite*; in
two books, respectively piano solo and piano duet.) This is
simple music but not trivial. It is written for young perfor-
mers; there are no technical difficulties but considerable
subtlety of rhythm and expression. There is some direct
reference to the Peter Rabbit books—most successfully in
the 'pit-pat-paddle-pat' of the Puddle-Ducks' goose-step
and in Mr Jeremy Fisher's bold leaps—but this is music
prompted by rather than illustrative of the stories. Dudley
Glass's music (*The Songs of Peter Rabbit.* Warne, 1951) is
pleasant enough and uncommonly well printed, but his
words are often feeble. Beatrix Potter would surely have had
a devastating comment on his 'toddle along the lane . . . but
toddle back home again'. The songs are also incorporated in
a musical play by the composer.

A more recent enterprise was the recording, by Vivien
Leigh and others, of four tales for a gramophone record
company.

The first translation of *Peter Rabbit* (into French) was
made by Victorine Ballon early in the Beatrix Potter story.
Since then, there have been translations into ten languages;
not enough titles have been translated, however, to satisfy
the demand. These little books, so like the English originals
in appearance and so unfamiliar in expression, have a charm

of their own. Mr Paul Jennings* has been inspired to frolic in characteristic fashion with such exotic creatures as Sophie Canétang, 'a Stendhal heroine, acutely analysing love with a cavalry officer and a *petit bourgeois*', and Meistres Tigi-Dwt.

To the Potter industry belong too the host of imitators, conscious or unconscious, who have with varying degrees of lack of success followed the physical pattern of the Peter Rabbit books without once capturing the spirit of the original. It is perhaps true to say that every artist who has clothed his animal characters in fancy dress has, however unwittingly, followed Beatrix Potter's lead. The strength of this tradition is the more remarkable when one remembers that her great contemporary Leslie Brooke left no artistic progeny. Of all the neo-Potters the only writer to achieve individual success is Alison Uttley, and her Little Grey Rabbit wins the reader's affection because she springs, as did Peter Rabbit, from a deep and affectionate understanding of country ways and traditions.

* *Next to Oddliness*, Max Reinhardt, 1955.

IX. Beatrix Potter's World

From time to time there is a campaign against the dressed-up-animal school of children's books and those who have never read them denounce Beatrix Potter's books for their cosy, sentimental view of life. Peter Rabbit, they say, does millions of pounds' worth of damage to farm crops, Samuel Whiskers destroys and spreads disease, Mr Tod is a pest. Beatrix Potter knew all this better than most of her critics. She was a practical farmer for thirty years and a realist all her life. She knew what was the probable fate of Peter Rabbit, and for what reason Pigling Bland goes to market. 'Nature, though never consciously wicked, has always been ruthless'*, she said, and she always shows that unsentimental detachment which marks the true countryman. She likes her own creations, but she never leaves her readers seriously in doubt about them. Mr Samuel Whiskers is an attractive rogue, but the reader learns, without distress, that Moppet and Mittens make a good living out of rat-catching. They catch 'dozens and dozens of them'. Children too are ruthless. Hearing of Tom Kitten's plight in *The Roly-Poly Pudding* for the first time, Carol White 'seemed to have no sentimental feelings about her hero's predicament at all'.† There is nothing cosy about Beatrix Potter's world. She depicts accurately 'that pleasant unchanging world of realism and romance, which in our northern clime is stiffened by hard weather, a tough ancestry, and the strength that comes from the hills'*.

It is that subtle mixture of 'realism and romance' which

* *Horn Book*, 1944. † *Books before Five*, p. 107.

makes the world of her imagining so vivid and memorable. 'Here', says Dorothy White about her daughter's reaction to *Tom Kitten*, 'was a comprehensive universe'* and it is the completeness and the consistency of her world that children unconsciously recognise and react to. Puzzling, sometimes frightening, things happen, but they happen within the framework of a known society. It is because the picture is so consistent and sharply realised that these stories become a part of the everyday life of those families in which they are shared between one generation and another. The stories are, in a fundamental sense, true; they are also equally basically good. The morality of Beatrix Potter is profound for all that is never stated.

It is given to only a few writers to add something to the total of experience. Beatrix Potter's creation of character is comparable in kind, though not in degree, to that of Dickens. Both had the power of drawing individuals who represented also a summary of experience. It is this timeless universal quality which has embedded Tom Kitten, Jemima Puddle-Duck and Pigling Bland deep in the hearts of those who have met them at the right time and in the right company. Such characters are not less original and memorable for being conveyed in a few words and a few lines.

An otherwise excellent teacher said to me once, 'That Beatrix Potter's a terrible woman, don't you think?' I didn't, but I knew what he meant. The mannered style and in particular the fondness for fine polysyllabic words have distressed many well-meaning people; although I have never known them to distress a child. (It should be added that most children ought first to encounter these books with the help of an adult reader.) Beatrix Potter's style is as much a part of her art as her painting or her characters;

* *Books before Five*, p. 23.

all the elements in her books are inseparable. She used words which seemed the best for the purpose. A well-known modern writer has given her opinion that had she lived today Beatrix Potter would have had to rewrite the stories. What publisher would have dared to dictate to her? And one might as well try to rewrite an Elizabethan lyric! Beatrix might quote, with sufficient humility: 'What I have written I have written.'

Miss Rumer Godden dealt with the alleged 'difficulty' of Beatrix Potter in a delightful set of letters, purporting to be exchanged between the writer—or rather her ghost—and an American publisher, which appeared in *Horn Book* in August 1963. This light-hearted essay conceals the finest critical appreciation of Beatrix Potter as a writer which has so far appeared.

Everyone who loves Beatrix Potter loves and remembers the pictures; her prose is often taken for granted when it is not condemned. She was in fact as great a master of word as of line. The mannerisms are always calculated; they give an atmosphere of formality and elegance where the mood of the story needs it. In ordinary narrative she is clean and economical, never a word too many and every one in its place. She is particularly successful in dialogue, which is beautifully expressed and always coloured by the characters of the speakers. There are obvious advantages in being one's own illustrator; equally it helps for an illustrator to be her own author. Drawing is a slow process compared with writing, and while putting in the perfections of detail in her pictures Beatrix had ample time to ponder her story and to distil the fine essence of every word.

At least one generation of readers has been brought up on inadequate reproductions of the drawings, although efforts have now been made to improve the standard.

The Art of Beatrix Potter, however, revealed what had

only been suspected, that here was an artist of extraordinary virtuosity. She never managed to draw humans, but in animal and flower drawing, in landscape and architecture she was a master. Her landscapes, for example 'Kirkcudbright Bay' in *The Art of Beatrix Potter*, are in the main stream of the English water-colour. She disliked critics who compared her with the great names of English painting, but in her miniature way that is where she belongs. The most accessible of her originals (*The Tailor of Gloucester*) are in the Tate Gallery—where they face somewhat incongruously the splendidly erotic 'Königsmark' drawings of Rex Whistler. In them it is possible to study her strength and her limitations: the loving appreciation of fine old furniture, the texture of cloth and china, the kindly, shrewd drawings of animals, so true to their own natures even in fancy dress, the immature drawing (after Caldecott) of the tailor, the skilled selection of detail and of aspect.

Whatever pleasure there may be in examining the exquisite detail of these books, however, it is their total effect which matters. This results from a unique combination of observation, fine craftsmanship and a rich humane sense of values. The books 'have been written out of an environment known and loved, and to which they are true'*, says Mrs Miller, and it is in this fundamental truth that their essential virtue lies. Mrs Dorothy White writes, 'The Potter books . . . could compose a tiny child's library. If he read nothing else, he would have experienced in them the basic human types and the basic human emotions—but more than that, what tremendous fun he would have.'† It was fun that Beatrix Potter sought to give; being herself, to fun she added, almost involuntary, truth and integrity.

* *Horn Book*, 1941.
† *About Books for Children*, by Dorothy Neal White. Oxford University Press, p. 44.

x. Peter Rabbit Conquers the World

Beatrix Potter was a product of English society and her books were prompted by and mirrored the English country scene. Nearly all of them belong to a small area in the Lake District. The characters speak a characteristic and mannered English, at once colloquial and elegant. We know that the children of Sawrey loved the books, seeing in them familiar scenes and people. English children who have never visited Sawrey, have never seen a fox or a red squirrel, who have seen ducks and rats only briefly and in unfamiliar settings, have taken the stories to their hearts because the language is both familiar and strange and the idiom of the pictures belongs to a tradition in which they grow.

What of Beatrix Potter in other countries? Most of my copies of her books bear prices in rupees. At a time when because of wartime restriction they were rarely to be found in English bookshops I bought them on Chowringhee in Calcutta. What were Bengali children making of the adventures of Tom Kitten?

There is abundant evidence that the books are loved in many parts of the world. A librarian in Lund writes, 'Swedish children like the books . . . very much, especially the two small picture books of Kune Nötpigg (a squirrel) and Elle Kanin (a rabbit). The clear and realistic pictures appeal to them, as does the short text which quite follows the picture . . . At story-hours at the library also the riddles in Kune Nötpigg have amused them very much.' The same story is told in Holland, but from both countries come complaints that too few of the books are translated and that even these are 'for long periods out of print'.

It is in America that Beatrix Potter has her most devoted following. There may be no obvious language difficulty here, although the tailor's 'I am worn to a ravelling' must be a foreign language in Chicago or New York. The social setting of the stories is surely completely alien to American readers. The American books which English children most enjoy, those by Laura Ingalls Wilder, Elizabeth Coatsworth and Elizabeth Enright, for example, are read by children old enough to see in them a picture of an unfamiliar country and its way of life. They are enjoyed *because* the setting is unfamiliar. American children meet Beatrix Potter long before they are capable of this critical approach. It is the universal, not the local, quality in Beatrix Potter which captures her readers.

There is no sign that this appeal is weakening. Miss Sarah Fenwick from Chicago says, 'More children are familiar with at least a few of the Potter books today than ever before.' And the same writer quotes librarians as saying, 'Oh, my yes, the children borrow and read and enjoy as many copies as we can provide.'

From Pittsburgh comes news of a permanent Beatrix Potter display in the Children's Library. A friend of the library presented a set of figurines of some of the characters and commissioned a local artist, Miss Jean Thoburn to design a setting for them. Miss Thoburn visited England to make drawings in the Beatrix Potter country and took the greatest trouble to get authentic details. As a result, Pittsburgh now has three lighted showcases built into the bookshelves, in which children can see their favourite books brought vividly to life. The scenes are: a street from *The Tailor of Gloucester*, the interior of Hill Top Farm, showing Tom Kitten's stove, and Mr McGregor's garden. 'The perspective in each picture is amazing,' says Miss Virginia Chase, the Head of Boys and Girls Department. 'Our children do enjoy the Beatrix Potter books and want the stories read over and over again.'

Miss Margaret Clark, of the Lewis Carroll Room in Cleveland Public Library, confirms this interest among American children. 'Of all Beatrix Potter's stories, *The Tale of Peter Rabbit* is most popular with the children in Cleveland as it probably is everywhere children are introduced to the tiny book treasures. . . . The choice, fully detailed little sketches, the animals reacting like small children, and the just but amusing plight of poor Peter . . . are all wonderfully appealing to little children.' Part of the charm of Beatrix Potter, in America as in England, is that in these books the generations meet on equal terms. 'Many parents and even grandparents recall a particular character that won their childhood affection and are eager to share it with their own children. Many times we have been asked to identify the books in which such characters appeared. . . . About a decade ago we compiled an index of all Beatrix Potter's characters just to meet such calls, and it has been worth its weight in gold.'

In Boston, too, the books have their following. Miss Virginia Haviland, formerly Readers' Adviser for Children there, speaks of the delight that Boston children find in the miniature precision of the books. 'The stories are so perfect in their little adventures and exact details (all the foods described, the costumes, and the small households) . . . My own library experience has furnished me with repeated cases of small children who demand over and over again the same one of the books, to the dismay of the parents who would like a change of read-aloud diet.'

In Boys and Girls House in Toronto, long the home of

some of the best library work with children in the world, Beatrix Potter is to be found. 'Canadian children take Miss Moppet to bed with them, name their own pets after Samuel Whiskers, beam from ear to ear when Peter Rabbit is mentioned, and rush in from playing to tell their mothers that "Squirrel Nutkin is out in our garden right now",' says Miss Jean Thomson. Miss Thomson stresses the lasting appeal of the books. In England, as in Toronto, an 'eleven-year-old will take one home obviously to renew acquaintance with a favourite character, but usually with a mumbled excuse about a small brother or sister at home'. A spot-check in two libraries in Toronto revealed that out of between three and four hundred copies of Beatrix Potter books in stock only thirty to forty were on the shelves. Miss Thomson comments, 'This is not our busy time of year and at these same libraries in March there will be days when the librarians will wish they had an extra dozen *Peter Rabbits*, for we all feel sorry when any child who wants a particular one of these books has to go home without it.'

It is clear that these most English of little books are also the most universal in appeal, for fundamentally they are concerned with qualities of character and behaviour which know no boundaries of time or place.

A BEATRIX POTTER
CHECK LIST

*Dates are given in square brackets when they do
not appear on the title-page of the original edition.*

The Tale of Peter Rabbit. Private edition [1901]. Warne [1902]
The Tailor of Gloucester. Private edition 1902. Warne, 1903
The Tale of Squirrel Nutkin. Warne, 1903
The Tale of Benjamin Bunny. Warne, 1904
The Tale of Two Bad Mice. Warne, 1904
The Tale of Mrs Tiggy-Winkle. Warne, 1905
The Pie and the Patty-Pan. Warne, 1905
The Tale of Mr Jeremy Fisher. Warne, 1906
The Story of Miss Moppet. Warne [1906]
The Story of a Fierce Bad Rabbit. Warne [1906]
The Tale of Tom Kitten. Warne, 1907
The Tale of Jemima Puddle-Duck. Warne, 1908
The Roly-Poly Pudding (later *The Tale of Samuel Whiskers*),
    Warne, 1908
The Tale of the Flopsy Bunnies. Warne, 1909
Ginger and Pickles. Warne, 1909
The Tale of Mrs Tittlemouse. Warne, 1910
Peter Rabbit's Painting Book. Warne, 1911
The Tale of Timmy Tiptoes. Warne, 1911
The Tale of Mr Tod. Warne, 1912
The Tale of Pigling Bland. Warne, 1913
Appley Dapply's Nursery Rhymes. Warne [1917]
Tom Kitten's Painting Book. Warne [1917]
The Tale of Johnny Town-Mouse. Warne [1918]
Cecily Parsley's Nursery Rhymes. Warne [1922]
Jemima Puddle-Duck's Painting Book. Warne [1925]
Peter Rabbit's Almanac for 1929. Warne [1928]
The Fairy Caravan. Private edition, 1929. Warne [1952]. Phila-
    delphia: McKay [1929]

The Tale of Little Pig Robinson. Warne [1930]. Philadelphia: McKay [1930]

Sister Anne, illustrated by Katherine Sturges. Philadelphia: McKay [1932]

Wag-by-Wall. Limited edition. Warne [1944]. Boston: *Horn Book*, 1944

The Tale of the Faithful Dove. Limited edition, Warne [1955], New York: Warne, 1956